Lebanon 24/7

adventure stories & travel guide

*You shall be free indeed when your days are not
without a care nor your nights without a want and a grief,
But rather when these things girdle your life and you
rise above them naked and unbound.*

Khalil Gibran, *The Prophet*

For my grandmother, a devoted traveller, Edith Giel-Van Hengel
(1932-2014)
For my dear parents Irma and Hans

Second (revised) edition (2018), adapted and translated from
the author's Dutch book 'Alle Dagen Libanon, van tricky
Tripoli tot bruisend Beiroet', published in 2016.

Author: Martijn van der Kooij
Translation: Diederik Rodenburg / Linda van Tilburg (chapter I)
Editor: Ayesha de Sousa
Publisher: Donald Suidman, BigBusinessPublishers, Utrecht
www.bbpublishers/lebanon
Cover design and map of Lebanon: Vincent Schenk
Book design: Studio Patrick, Rotterdam
Photo spread (page 2/3) and cover photo:
Ahmed Mouissaoui (Flickr.com)

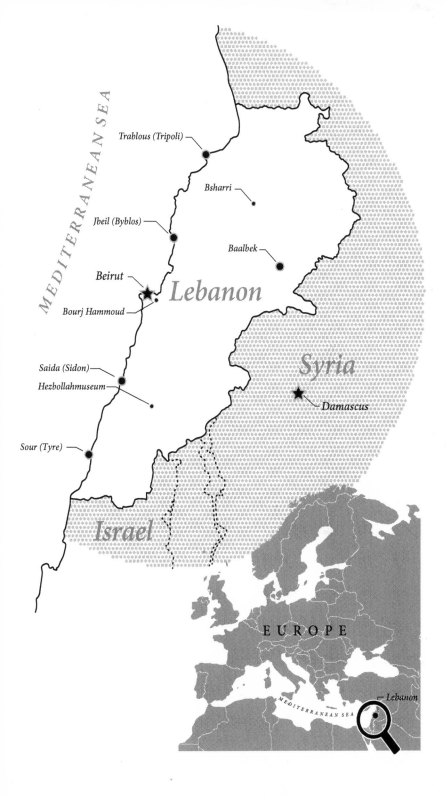

MEDITERRANEAN SEA

Trablous (Tripoli)

Bsharri

Jbeil (Byblos)

Baalbek

Beirut

Lebanon

Bourj Hammoud

Syria

Saida (Sidon)

Hezbollahmuseum

Damascus

Sour (Tyre)

Israel

EUROPE

MEDITERRANEAN SEA

Lebanon

Contents

Introduction

When I first set foot in Lebanon, there were many things I could never have imagined. At that time, I had hardly ever written about the Middle East as a Dutch reporter. As far as I remember, my story about 'things to do in Egypt', following a holiday in the Nile-country, was the closest I had come to it. When I arrived in Beirut in December 2012, an entirely new city to me, I didn't suspect that I would return countless times, even less that I would record my adventures in a book. And how could I have guessed that, in March 2017, I would practically move to Lebanon in order to write my books from a balcony overlooking the capital?

In September 2016, my stories about Lebanon were published in my Dutch book, '*Alle Dagen Libanon*'. My publisher had been sceptical about this project, thinking that this religiously diverse country would not spark much interest among the Dutch. Only its Civil War was still fresh in the minds of many of my compatriots, and ever since then, all the news coming out of Lebanon has been tragic: bombs exploding and politicians being murdered. Most people will remember the car bomb that killed Lebanese Prime Minister, Rafiq Hariri, in 2005 and the heavy bombing by Israel a year later (in retaliation for the rockets fired by Hezbollah). Because of Lebanon's negative image, my publisher didn't expect much interest in my adventure story book and travel guide.

He was proved wrong! The media were immediately drawn to the 'other side' of Lebanon, something with very different accounts from those that existed already. The book was well received, sold well (in its own niche market, admittedly) and for me, it resulted in many encounters in Lebanon with Dutch people who first read the book and then contacted me. Some of them even told me that it was my descriptions that had actually convinced them to buy a ticket. This made me embarrassed and proud at the same time.

I decided to not bring an exact translation of my Dutch book onto the international market. Readers had been requesting more photos and more tourist information, so that was the first change I made. I also included an epilogue, detailing how the main characters in this book have continued with their lives three years on. And finally, I decided to rewrite my introduction on Lebanon. I wanted it to be more thorough and more informative. But I didn't want to take any sides. My introduction had to be strictly objective, free of my personal opinions.

And this is where my problem began. Because how can you produce a brief and neutral introduction to this tiny, but extremely complex country on the Mediterranean Sea? Lebanon has everything in one place: rich and poor, Christian and Muslim, Phoenician and Arab, modern and conservative.

Let me start by giving an example. Ask any Lebanese person *who* was responsible for starting the Lebanese Civil War (1975-1990), *what* happened during those years and *who* finally won. You will get a wide range of answers. There is no single national narrative. History teachers at Lebanese schools do not even embark on this sensitive subject. Remember that many of the key players of the

War and their offspring are still active in today's Lebanese politics (the current President, Michel Aoun, for example, was a General in the Lebanese army).

What people know about this dark episode in Lebanon's history is what they have been told first-hand by their parents and grand-parents. And *their* perspective, most of the time, depends on their own religious or ethnic background.

I won't go too much into the detail of this great scar on Lebanese society, but what I have learned from reading eyewitness accounts like those of journalists Robert Fisk and Thomas E. Friedman, is that the war was essentially a power struggle. Not the kind I know from my country: power in the Netherlands is about shared decision-making and compromises. In the Middle East it's about winning and leaving your enemy empty-handed. The present war in Syria is the best example of that. Friedman uses the image of the egg and its shell. In the Middle East, you 'eat the egg with the shell', he wrote. You do not leave anything behind for your enemy: it's a game of 'all or nothing'.

The 18 sects of Lebanon

Lebanon is like a tapestry woven from different faiths. It counts 18 official religions that are recognised by the State and are known as 'sects'. The three major monotheistic world religions are repre-sented in the country, though the number of Jews in Lebanon has become insignificant. Those who did not emigrate after the crea-tion of Israel or after the Civil War, which destroyed the Jewish Quarter, live a clandestine life. I once met a man wearing the portrait of Saint Charbel around his neck. When my friend spoke to him in Arabic and made some reference to this Christian saint, (of whom my friend too, although Muslim, was an admirer), to our surprise our new acquaintance confided that he was actually Jewish and wore the medallion to protect his identity. Perhaps his ability to be so honest with us was helped by the fact that we were in an LGBTQI setting at the time. I was flabbergasted, even though he was not the first Jew I met in Lebanon, as you will read in my stories. It's common for Lebanese Jews to hide their identity out of fear of being seen by the outside world as a spy for Israel, a country that is still officially at war with Lebanon. According to the chairman of the Lebanese Jewish Community Council, Isaac Arazi, the community comprises around two thousand souls. The Council has an active Facebook account which gives Judaism a face in Lebanon.

Officially, Christianity is the biggest sect in terms of the number of adherents. However, this figure comes from the last census that was taken back in 1932 (!) while Lebanon was under a French mandate (1923-1946). The outcome – 51 percent Christian – might have been correct, but it is dubious. While on Mount Lebanon, Christians no doubt had an overwhelming majority (this is still true today), this was not the case in the northern city of Tripoli and in the captial Beirut.

The diversity among Lebanese Christians reflects the nature of the country. Almost all the Christian denominations are represented. The Maronites, an eastern branch that falls under the authority of the Vatican, constitute the largest group. Second, is the Eastern-Orthodox Church, whose followers are generally known to be wealthy. This Church adheres to the Greek-Orthodox patriarch in Antioch. The Melkite Christians (close to the Catholic Church) are in third place, followed by many smaller groups, including Protestants, Syrian-Orthodox and the Assyrian Church of the East.

Islam was brought to Lebanon in the 7th century by Arab tribes. Without a doubt, Lebanese Muslims form a majority of the population these days, but far from a unit. To understand the difference between the two main groups, Sunni and Shia, it is important to know the position of Ali, cousin and son-in-law of the prophet Mohamed. The Shiite Muslims claim that Ali was the rightful successor to Mohamed, thus leader (imam) of the Muslim community. However, Ali was assassinated in 661. His sons, Hassan and Hussein, were not allowed to rule the caliphate. Another difference with the Sunni is that most Shiite Muslims are awaiting the return of the 'hidden imam', Al Mahdi. He is said to never have died and will appear again just before the end of time.

Sunni Islam has a strong base in Saudi-Arabia, while Iran is the biggest Shia country. Backed by these two oil giants, the two religious groups have fought many wars against each other. As I write this introduction, Sunni and Shiite Muslims are slaughtering one another on the battlefields of Syria and Yemen. Though Lebanon as a country has mainly stayed out of these conflicts, the Lebanese Shiite militia and political party, Hezbollah (literally 'the Party of God'), sends its fighters to assist Syrian President, Bashar al-Assad. His regime has its base in the Alawi (a Shia sect) region of Latakia. Since March 2011, when the uprising in Syria began, the Sunni-Shia rivalry was a major source of tension within Lebanese society. The Sunni party, Future Movement, led by Prime Minister Saad Hariri, strongly opposes Hezbollah's actions in Syria. The Christian political movements are split into two blocs: those for Syria/ Hezbollah, and those against it. Didn't I warn you that Lebanon is a complex country?

The Civil War
If the Lebanese cannot agree on one unanimous version of what happened during the Civil War, how can you expect one from a foreigner? Let me give you an idea of the ingredients that ignited

the war in 1975, knowing of course that this is by no means the complete picture. It is important to know that at the time of the Ottoman Empire, Christians in Mount Lebanon had an autonomous semi-position most of the time. I looked into the official document that created the French Mandate, to see if the Maronites had been promised this position again after the collapse of the Ottoman Empire. This was not the case. 'Respect for the personal status of the various peoples and for their religious interest shall be fully guaranteed', says the League of Nations document. However, remember that according to the last census in 1932, Christians formed the majority.

An agreement, the National Pact, was signed by the various religious groups in 1943, setting out the balance of power in the newly-independent Lebanese State. Since fifty-one percent of the population was (supposedly) Christian, the National Pact stipulated that the presidency would be in the hands of this group. However, being Christian was not the only requirement for the post; the President needed to be a Maronite as well. It was further agreed that the Prime Minister should be a Sunni Muslim and the Speaker of Parliament, Shia. This situation is still in effect today. The Prime Minister back then was appointed by the President, which gave the latter even more power. In the Parliament Christians formed a majority, allowing them to veto any decision. After the Civil War, the power of the President was decreased and Christians lost their parliamentary majority, but still fifty percent of all parliamentary seats are allocated to this sect. However, due to a lot of division internally, there is no big Christian bloc in the parliament.

On 22 November 1943 Lebanon became independent. Soon after, in 1948, the country faced its first crisis. Palestinian refugees fleeing their homes from present day Israel arrived in Lebanon and

Jordan. Their number increased with the Arab-Israeli Six Day War in 1967. Around 400.000 people in total took refuge in Lebanon. They were not entitled to Lebanese citizenship – still the case today – and lived in special camps. The Palestinian Liberation Organisation (PLO) became militarily and politically active in these camps from the 1960s onwards. In 1970, the PLO established its headquarters in Beirut, having been expelled from Jordan. The goal of the organisation was to destroy the Jewish State, but since the PLO was based in Beirut, according to Friedman, its focus shifted increasingly to Lebanon, the (dire) situation in the Palestinian camps and the rights and interests of Palestinians in general.

In the time between Lebanese independence in 1943 and the start of the Civil War in 1975, the Lebanese government, dominated by Christians, was pro-Western while many leftists groups (such as the PLO) sympathised with the communist Soviet Union and the Pan-Arab movement. Sunnis in general were unhappy with their secondary position on the political battlefield, since it was widely known that they outnumbered the Christians (especially considering that Palestinians are primarily Sunni). The Shiite parties did not wield much power at all.

These and many more religious and political tensions built up and eventually culminated in the outbreak of the Civil War on 13 April 1975, when unidentified gunmen in a car attacked a church, killing four people. Later that day, Christian gunmen opened fire on a busload of Palestinians, in the same Orthodox Christian district of Ain al-Rameneh (Beirut). Thirty bus passengers were killed. During a bus ride, my Lebanese friend, Tofik, once pointed out the site of the 'bus massacre', as the incident is referred to these days. It made me take a deep breath and swallow, as I thought about the seemingly endless sectarian violence that would follow, with 120.000 casualties and at least 750.000 people displaced. It's still an open wound in Lebanese society.

The rise of Hezbollah

The French Mandate had little consideration for the Shia population, the third largest religious denomination. After Lebanon's independence they were given breadcrumbs in the power sharing set-up. In 1985, the appearance on the national stage of Hezbollah changed all of this. The 'Party of God' started as a mainly Shiite resistance movement against the Israeli occupation of Lebanon. It played an important role in chasing Israeli troops off Lebanese soil. Iranian money, excellent training and zealous faith made Hezbollah a fearless guerrilla force.

It's a misconception that Hezbollah is just a militia. In Shiite regions in Lebanon (Baalbek, villages in the Beqaa Valley and in South-Lebanon), it is also a social movement, which administrates schools and hospitals. This is how the group won its popularity mostly amongst the poor and neglected people in these regions. Last but not least, Hezbollah is a religious movement with Hassan Nasrallah as its leader.

If you follow international media you might be made to believe that all of Lebanon stands squarely behind Hezbollah, which the US has labelled a terrorist organisation. In reality, it occupies 12 seats (out of 128) since the parliamentary elections of 6 May 2018. Another 10 independent members of parliament are allied with the Shiite movement. Hezbollah has been enjoying a more comfortable position since the last elections, because a majority of the parties supports the main points of their political agenda. Their most powerful ally is the Christian Free Patriotic Movement, the country's biggest political party. Thus, the American, Saudi and Israeli ambition of disarming the military wing of Hezbollah seems to be an unlikely scenario in the coming years.

Hezbollah has widened its support base in recent years due to its operations in Syria against (Sunni) Islamic extremists

Who are the Druze?

You can find this minority group in mountainous areas to the east and south of Beirut. The Druze, who make up around five percent of the Lebanese population (250.000 people), also live in Syria and northern Israel. It's well-known that you should not antagonise a Druze. In this book I mention one of the many stories that illustrates this adage (see chapter IV).

Although the Druze religion is secret, we know that they believe in a single deity and in reincarnation. A Druze will be reborn as a Druze. They do not fast during Ramadan, have no mosques and women are not obliged to wear a *hijab* (headscarf). The Druze religion is regarded in Lebanon as a part of Islam.

Long-time Druze leader, Walid Jumblatt, now succeeded by his son, Taymur, is a free spirit. He has lobbied many times for the decriminalisation of cannabis and is a great lover of animals, especially dogs (which are considered *'haram'* – forbidden – in Islam). His Twitter account is witty and draws lots of attention.

If you come across men wearing oversized trousers, a small white hat on their head and a thick moustache, you are probably in the presence of a Druze man. He may be accompanied by a woman in a white *hijab* that covers her chin, neck and hair. But it's not very common to see this, as only the initiated Druze (less than ten percent) are allowed to dress in this manner. The Druze people protect themselves by only giving a small minority access to knowledge of their secret religion. You cannot convert to become a Druze and Druze are not allowed to marry non-Druze.

groups. Many Lebanese people have told me that it is thanks to Hezbollah operations in cooperation with the Syrian regime and the Russians that Lebanon has never come under serious threat of being invaded by ISIS and Al-Nusra. Shia and Christian villages on the border have also benefitted from the protection of Hezbollah against invasions by extremists.

After the Civil War it was agreed that Hezbollah was the only militia that would be allowed to retain its weapons. The idea was that the Shiite 'resistance group' would free Lebanon from the last remnants of Israeli occupation (Israel denies this). Also it was considered prudent at that time to keep Hezbollah in arms in case Israel invaded Lebanon once more. The country's own army was extremely weak then, so from a national security point of view, this was a logical step. However, after much reinforcement by the US, France, Saudi Arabia and other countries (including the Netherlands), the Lebanese national army has regained strength in the last decade, and is considered to be the best functioning State institution in the country. The US has declared that, despite Hezbollah's growing political domination, it will continue its support of the Lebanese Armed Forces.

Who are the Lebanese?

'We are Phoenicians, not Arabs'. It's a claim you will hear often if you spend time in Beirut. In this way the Lebanese have drawn a line between themselves and the surrounding Arab world. After all, aren't they descended from the ancient Phoenicians, a civilisation that created one of the first alphabets and left its traces in the old town of Byblos? It's a widely-held belief, particularly among Christians. At Beirut airport, notably, the distinction is made. Before the customs and immigration desk, a sign instructs 'Arabs' to use the right lane and 'Lebanese', the left. This strikes me every time I enter the country.

The Lebanese also differentiate themselves from their Arab neighbours by their language. A common greeting is illustrative of this: '*Hi, kifak, ça va*'? '*Kifak*' is Lebanese for 'how are you?' And there is much more. *Bonjour* and *bonsoir* are often used and have even been altered to '*bonjoureen*' and '*bonsoireen*', where the Arabic plural 'een' is added to wish somebody more than one good day or evening. French visitors are often tickled by this distortion of their language the first time they hear it.

As complex as the country is, the Lebanese seem to live a simple life, not one run by a schedule filled with carefully-made appointments, like many people in the northern hemisphere. In this way, the Lebanese are similar to southern Europeans. They do not like to plan things far ahead of time. Many social gatherings are spontaneously arranged the same day. A lot of free time is spent with family. Especially on Sundays, when most people are off work, family lunches are held in the parental home.

Divorce was a big taboo in Lebanese society, but this has changed in the last decade. Still today, there is no civil marriage, so those who require a non-religious ceremony get married in nearby Cyprus and register the marriage in Lebanon afterwards. For many, this happens out of necessity, because Lebanese religious authorities do not accept mixed marriages.

Party life

Beirut's nightlife is world famous as the Lebanese are fond of partying. And this does not include only young people. In restaurants with live Arab music, you can find a mixed crowd and at the end of the night, everyone takes to the dance floor. Lebanon is famous in the Arab world for its musicians. Fayrouz, the 'Cedar of Lebanon' is the pride of the nation. She made her breakthrough in

1957 at the Baalbeck International Music Festival and has been the most successful Lebanese singer ever since.

Also unique in the region is the high level of education in Lebanon. This is a vestige of the pre-war time. There is a wide variety of private schools and universities, and State education also provides a good basis for students. Most well-known is the American University of Beirut (founded in 1866), whose buildings on the shore of Beirut are worth a visit in themselves. Because of the excellent level of education, many Lebanese graduates find work in the Gulf (Dubai, Kuwait, Qatar, etc.) or in Africa. This contributes to the growing number of expats. Currently 13 million people of Lebanese origin are living outside the country, while Lebanon only has 4.5 million citizens.

Not a typical place in the Middle East
If you have specific wishes, you will not be disappointed in Beirut and its surroundings. If you are gay, you will find plenty of places that attract an LGBTQI crowd. Do you love gambling? Drive out of Beirut to the north and after twenty minutes, on your left, you will see the famous 'Casino du Liban'. Besides this luxurious venue, it is not difficult to find a gambling hall in Lebanon. And let's not forget one of the biggest Arab attractions in Lebanon before Dubai was developed: these men-only clubs feature dancing girls from Eastern European countries. In Lebanon they are known as 'super night clubs', but a better word would be brothels.

This brings me to what many people have in mind when they refer to Beirut as the 'Paris of the Middle East'. There are still traces of a city that might have resembled Paris. Vibrant and fresh, Beirut has retained some of its splendour. However, since the fifties, when the term 'Paris of the Middle East' was coined and Lebanon was regularly flooded with European tourists, many things have changed. The camps constructed by Palestinian refugees have grown into shantytowns. The Civil War destroyed cultural heritage all over the country and there has been a massive exodus of Lebanese people to safer places. The 2006 war with Israel was short-lived but caused most of its damage on the Lebanese side: bridges, roads and power stations were destroyed. And since 2011 more than one million Syrian people have found refuge in Lebanon. The country has almost collapsed under this weight: so many new mouths to feed, children to educate and even more strain on employment levels. Added to all of this, the country suffers from a severe electricity shortage and an excess of (household) waste.

The spirit of Lebanon

Astonishingly, despite all of its problems, 'the spirit of Lebanon' has always survived. It is what makes Lebanon special. It's not southern Italy or Greece, even though it bears strong resemblances to these countries, and it is also very different from all other Arab countries. Lebanese people enjoy life to the fullest, tend to take the law with a pinch of salt and, while still attached to family and tradition, are more open-minded and progressive than neighbouring Arab States.

Sadly enough, it is also the only country in the Middle East where religious diversity still exists on this scale. Where else can eighteen religious groups (in practice even more, because the eighteen only includes those that are recognised by the government) live together? Where in the Arab world would you find Armenian people holding a mass celebration in a football stadium in honour of Armenian Independence Day (with alcohol, fireworks and shows), while at the same time many Muslims are fasting for Ramadan? And which other city has a Sunni mosque standing next to a Maronite cathedral, both within walking distance of a synagogue? Muslims pay visit to the Virgin Mary on the Harissa hilltop and Sunni members of parliament support the Shiite Hezbollah. These are some of the surprising facets of this diverse nation.

Is it safe?

Oh, you still have one important question? The one everybody asks me? Whether Lebanon is a safe place to visit. 'No, it isn't', is my standard answer. 'The traffic over there is like a killing machine. Very dangerous.' People usually laugh at this, but they understand my point. Have I ever felt unsafe? Yes, I have. In 2013, a year when Lebanon was on the brink of destabilisation: bombs exploded in the Shiite neighbourhood of Dahieh, prominent politicians were assassinated and the portraits, on Sassine Square, of Lebanese bishops who had gone missing in Syria, reminded me of how close the war was. I considered leaving the country – but I didn't. And in the years that followed, I kept coming back. The situation was getting steadily better just as, ironically, ISIS-led terror attacks were becoming more frequent in Europe. With my dark Dutch sense of humour I sometimes told people that I was happy to be safe in Lebanon rather than in Paris or London. Bad jokes aside, the truth is that Lebanon is in calmer waters.

With all of this said, I can only urge you to see Lebanon for yourself. Taste the best food in the Middle East, drink excellent domestically-produced wine, visit the ancient souq of Saida (Sidon) and enjoy the beautiful shores of Sour (Tyre). The Baalbek temples will be among the most magnificent constructions you have ever seen and the Lebanese will welcome you warmly to their country: *Ahla wa sahla bi Loubnen* (welcome to Lebanon)!

Facts about Lebanon

POPULATION
Lebanese: 4.5 - 5 million people
Palestinians: 174.000 people[*]
Syrians: 1 million people[**]

GDP: 47.54 billion USD (2016)[***]
GDP per capita: 6983 USD[***]

Area: 10.425 km2
Highest mountain: Qurnat as Sawda (3088 metres)

President: Michel Aoun (Free Patriotic Movement, Christian)
Prime Minister: Saad Hariri (Future Movement, Sunni)
Speaker of the House: Nabih Berri (Amal, Shia)

National food: hummus (white chickpea dip), kibbe (meat-balls), falafel (deep-fried chickpea balls), fattoush (fresh salad with mint, lemon, sumac berries), tabouleh (parsley and bulgur wheat salad), moutabal (aubergine dip) and much more!
Currency: Lebanese Pound (Lira in Arabic) 1500 LBP = 1 USD, fixed rate. US Dollars are welcome everywhere

* *Latest census by the Lebanese-Palestinian Dialogue Commission in 2017. Registered at UNWRA: more than 500.000 Palestinians*
** *Registered Syrian refugees dropped under 1 million in 2017 according to the UN. The number of unregistered Syrians is unknown.*
*** *Source: Trading Economics/ World Bank*

I In Beirut

On 15 December 2012 I took my very first steps on Lebanese soil. At last, a dream I had cherished most of my life was coming true. Lebanon had been the country of my childhood nights. In the eighties my parents started their evenings with the news bulletin, and as a boy, I joined them in this ritual. Night after night, while sipping my pre-bedtime warm milk and gingerbread, I watched as buildings turned into skeletons. In the background the gunfire of snipers ricocheted while people ran across streets for shelter, for dear life. This was Beirut during the Civil War, constantly on the international news in those days. At the time I had no understanding of what I was witnessing, but the images stuck in my mind as I grew older. Through the years, my curiosity about Beirut grew. I yearned to travel to Lebanon to discover the country and its capital with my own eyes. What had become of this city, this nation, the people I had seen huddling to escape the snipers, more than twenty years after the end of the bloody Civil War?

It took a long time for my dream to come true. Not by choice. In 2006, I had firm travel plans in place when the Lebanese Hezbollah movement (literally 'Party of God') showered rockets onto Israel. The Southern neighbour's brutal retaliation struck Lebanon heavily. Apart from military targets and civil 'Hezbollah areas', the Israeli fire also destroyed bridges and power plants. Once again, Lebanon was left in darkness, in a very literal sense.

The media famously portrayed the young Lebanese jet set driving through the battered capital in a sporty red convertible, flaunting trendy sunglasses and expensive outfits, the wind in their hair. The war with Israel caused me to cancel my trip, but this odd cliché caught my attention and intrigued me even more. I had to go to Beirut, no matter what.

Everything went smoothly once I landed at the small, modern Rafiq Hariri airport. The signs at customs seemed absurd to me: Lebanese in the left lane, Arabs in the right. As if Lebanese people weren't Arabs. It was only later that I discovered that many Lebanese people feel Phoenician, claiming as their ancestors the Phoenicians who inhabited the land from 1500 BC. This learned group settled in the city of Byblos, north of Beirut, and developed one of the world's first alphabets (which forms the basis of our alphabet). Recent DNA research has proved the Lebanese right; the majority are indeed genetically related to the Phoenicians, rather than to the Arabs. A collective sigh of relief was breathed all over Lebanon when this news broke.

From my past travels through Egypt I had found taxi drivers in the Arab world to be lying, cheating thieves. Once, in Cairo, a driver told me he had no change, but only after taking my banknotes. He then forced me out of the car. So I arrived in Beirut as a cautious man, to say the least. I ignored the men shouting 'taxi, taxi' in the arrival hall (who tend to be the crooks) and went outside to the official taxi rank. There I found a driver who said he knew my hotel and offered a fair price to take me there. Off we drove, into the busy late night traffic, in a 'free style' that immediately reminded me of Egypt. It was my first experience of what I later realised were the driving rules of every Lebanese driver: overtake from the left or right on the highway? Fine. Take up two lanes? Be our guest. Force your priority at a crossroad? Sure, if your car is bigger than the others, that's your right. Indeed nobody follows the actual rules, neither in traffic nor in anything else for that matter. My driver was very talkative. He spoke elementary French and sometimes used a few English words. He couldn't get over the fact that I had chosen Lebanon as my holiday destination. *'Pourquoi Liban? Pourquoi?'* he kept repeating. Ordinary Lebanese workers like him can't imagine foreigners visiting their country by choice.

From the airport the road led us through the Hezbollah 'controlled' district of Dahieh, to the heart of the city. When I spotted the famous mosque with the blue domes which was beautifully depicted on the cover of my travel guide, I knew we had reached the centre and that my hotel wouldn't be far now. The final leg however, took longer than the drive from airport to the city. At a snail's pace the car crept through a street bursting with bars, restaurants and nightclubs that all looked very inviting. Double-parked vehicles and a constant flow of cars trying to enter or leave a parking space, meant that we came to a halt every few metres. The air was filled with the noise of impatient tooting from the line of cars. I didn't see the red convertible with the jet set youngsters, but what I did see was everything I had dreamed Beirut to be: energetic, alive, a city that never sleeps. The taxi driver pointed out a few nightclubs that had an entrance fee of about a hundred dollars (I found out later that he wasn't exaggerating). He didn't drop me off in front of my hotel. That was complicated, he said. Little did I know then that a lot of things were complicated in this country. I meekly accepted his directions and starting walking, to find out that my driver had not been lying to me – on the contrary. When I arrived at my hotel, I realised the one-way traffic would have forced the taxi to take a huge detour that, in this traffic, would easily have lost him an hour.

On top of that, the entrance turned out to be in a small, pedestrian side street of the charming Rue Pasteur. A sign instructed visitors to go down the stone steps for the 'Saifi Urban Gardens'. On the steps I heard lively Arabic music. A band was performing in Em Nazih, the vibrant café next door. A young crowd was dancing; everywhere you could smell the *shisha*, the water pipe. Almost none of the women wore a *hijab*, while most men sported a fashionable barber-trimmed beard. Now I really felt I was in Lebanon. The man in the hotel lobby handed me the key to my room, which turned out to be exactly thirty steps from the café's dance floor. Yet I fell asleep quickly, exhausted from my trip, the Arabic music rocking me as I drifted off. I felt euphoric – overwhelmed by how surreal it was. At the same time things couldn't get any more real than this. I was in Beirut, at last.

II 'Samira' to his friends

Waking up in a strange city is a thrilling experience. Opening my eyes, I hardly knew where I was. The ground floor room in which I had arrived the previous night in the dark looked quite different now with the sun bouncing off the walls. It was large and scantily furnished: just two single beds, a wardrobe and a small desk with a tiny shower and washstand in one corner. The windows were barred, which, strangely enough, made me feel quite safe. What struck me was the absence of glass in the window frames. A little while later I found that there were shutters that could be pulled closed if one reached through the bars. My room looked over a very small courtyard packed with a great deal of junk: old chairs, tables, barrels and gas canisters.

It was a beautiful December day and as I walked out of the hotel at about eleven that morning I looked up at the deep blue sky, noting that the winter sun had not lost its strength. A t-shirt, jeans and a summer jacket kept me warm enough. I walked past the Em Nazih café where the night before a live band had entertained a crowd of youngsters. It was very quiet there now. A small number of fash-ionably-dressed young people were sucking on their water pipes. I sat down under the canvas and noticed a huge bus depot directly opposite the open-air café. It was a concrete complex consisting of three floors and it explained the smell of diesel oil I had detected when I woke up that morning. At breakfast, which was included in the arrangement, I was given the choice between two dishes both of which were completely unknown to me. I took a chance on the *manoushe*. An old-ish man began to prepare my food in an oven that sat in the corner of the terrace and within ten minutes I was served a plate of warm flat bread, folded in half and filled with melted cheese. This much-loved delicacy is served fresh off the baking tray and is eaten with a wide choice of accompaniments. On a well-satisfied stomach, I began my first exploratory walk, checking out the area around the hotel, as I always do on arrival in unfamiliar territory. The district where I was staying, Gemmayze, is an absolute gem. It embodied what I imagined to be the Beirut of before the civil war: its streets boasting French names that echoed the French style of the houses. Some of the houses appeared to be in a better state than others, but the overall effect was very impressive. The main street, Rue Gouraud, was as flat as a Dutch polder while the side streets were steep, leading up a hill and could only be entered by climbing steps. The broad steps were painted in rainbow colours and were reminiscent of the ones I had seen in the district of Lapa in Rio de Janeiro. Even now, in winter, there were plants in full bloom. And everywhere I looked there were cafés, restaurants, nightclubs and discotheques. I spent my first day looking for buildings riddled with bullet holes, fallen-in roofs and other such remnants of the Civil War. But I soon found that large areas of the city which had been damaged were brilliantly restored, virtually erasing the scars of the war.

Following an afternoon of meandering through this new world, I was ready for my next adventure. That evening, I had arranged to get together with a Lebanese man whom I had met online. Two weeks before my trip, this man, nicknamed *Pax Vobis,* had sent me the following message: '*Ow nice close to my home saifi urban garden it's really a good place they teach Arabic too we can talk by whatsapp this is my number 4961170xxxo1*'. We chatted for a while on Whatsapp and I was curious to meet this twenty-six year-old who spoke both English and French and turned out to be very interested in politics. He had invited me to his home for a drink, which I gladly accepted. When I asked for his address, he told me that he would pick me up at my hotel, explaining that in his district of Bourj Hammoud, an Armenian quarter, addresses were quite difficult to find. I later discovered that street addresses are rarely used in Lebanon – people tend to meet each other near a mosque or a church. I gratefully accepted his offer and later that afternoon I was met by him and his friend, Rabih, who drove the car. My new friend's house was only a ten-minute drive away. He had an apartment on the twelfth floor with a beautiful view of the city, the mountains and a glimpse of the Mediterranean Sea. The house had a spacious living room, three bedrooms and on the roof terrace there was another bedroom, shower and kitchen. In the house I noticed flags hanging everywhere, Spanish, Moroccan, French and even Chinese. On the balcony a rainbow flag, with the word PACE (peace) in large letters, stood proudly. This banner, which was visible far into the city, is an international symbol (without the letters) of gay liberation. I was taken on a short tour of the flat and fell in love with it immediately. We settled ourselves on the spacious terrace overlooking the skyscrapers of Beirut, deep in conversation. There were only two of us now; Rabih had driven off in his car. Although it was December, it felt like a summer evening.

Elie was an energetic and a somewhat stout young man. At the time I met him, he was working as an assistant nurse in a hospital. Every morning, his parents picked him up at half past four and drove him to work where he stayed from five in the morning until three o'clock in the afternoon. To complement his earnings, Elie had a sizeable income by letting out two rooms in the house as well as the roof terrace studio. A Lebanese painter rented one of the rooms. I did not get to meet him that afternoon as he was having a nap. The other room was home to a German student who was at the university at that moment. Both tenants I would meet at a later stage. The apartment above Elie's was occupied by a Lebanese/ Dutch couple. I was very impressed by Elie's entrepreneurship. My new friend had a lot to tell me about Lebanon. By means of a map on the wall – which incidentally had Israel labelled as 'Palestine' – he told me of all the places I needed to visit, what to see and how I should get there. I was overwhelmed with all the information and just as I was about to leave, a man in his early forties entered the apartment. His beard, purple knitted cap and the big shawl covering his shoulders in spite of the warm weather made him look like a hippy. Curiously, instead of socks, plastic bags covered his feet and showed above his boots. His name was Tofik and to my amazement he introduced himself as Elie's boyfriend. What was more astonishing was that they lived together in what struck me as blatant defiance of the mores of the Middle East. I wondered what the neighbours thought.

Two days later I was on my way back to Bourj Hammoud. Elie had invited me to a Christmas party together with some of his friends. I had decided to walk, assuming that I would easily find Elie's apartment again. That task, however, turned out to be a little more difficult than I had anticipated. When I arrived in the Armenian quarter I ended up in a maze of identical streets and alleyways. I sent a desperate text message to Elie who advised me to take a taxi to 'Knesset al-Inaye' where he would collect me. Later on, he said how amused he had been by my Hebrew pronunciation of the word 'knesset', because in Lebanese Arabic the letter 't' is not articulated, while the 'e' sounds more like an 'i'. So in Lebanese *knesset* is pronounced *'knisseh'*. It must have sounded as if I were asking the way to the Knesset, the Israeli parliament!

Apparently, there were quite a number of churches in this neighbourhood, because my taxi driver had to ask several people the way to the *Knesset al-Inaye*. After a thirty-minute drive through this lively neighbourhood (traffic was very slow due to the Christmas rush), I was dropped off at the entrance of the church where Elie was waiting. As we walked together towards his apartment, I felt I could have kicked myself: I recognised the junkyard that we had passed the previous day without recognising the building containing Elie's apartment.

Elie did not seem to mind my late arrival in the least. It was only about 8 o'clock and a few of his friends were busy in the kitchen, making a salad called 'tabouleh'. It seemed quite a job; all the parsley leaves needed to be cut from the roots. Rabih, who I had met the previous day in the car, was busy setting up the enormous sound equipment in the living room. Presents had been laid out under the Christmas tree, which itself had been decorated with red and green twinkling lights. Tofik sat on the floor, still wearing his knitted hat, working on his laptop and oblivious to the hustle and bustle around him. I found him rather strange.

By about nine, all the guests had arrived and we sat around the dinner table, wearing the Christmas hats that Elie had bought for us. It was quite a jolly sight. The food was laid out on the table all at once. No separate courses here. An unbelievable amount of food was put in front of me, containing mostly unfamiliar ingredients. There was especially a lot of meat, which, as a vegetarian, I didn't touch.

Luckily, there were enough vegetarian dishes too: salads, pastries filled with spinach, grilled haloumi cheese and Lebanese bread. As far as the beverages were concerned, vodka was the clear favourite although wine was also in high demand.

The entire evening buzzed with rumours of the 'surprise' that Elie had in store for us. At about eleven o'clock a choir of some fifty Filipinos, half of them children, assembled in the room. Just before their performance, Elie gave a short account of the often dire conditions suffered by foreign workers in Lebanon and that he, Elie, had managed to find this wonderful choir with the help of an international organisation which fought for the rights of these people. The room was soon filled with the sound of Christmas classics which permeated the street through the open balcony doors. In the Netherlands, neighbours would have called the police immediately; here the neighbours didn't seem bothered by it. After *Jingle Bells* had been sung again in Filipino as an encore, the singers went round the room with a hat and then were on their way to their next gig. After the concert, Elie's friends jovially cheered 'Samira, Samira!!!' I had heard that name constantly throughout the evening but I hadn't been able to identify its bearer. I did see Elie's sister, Rima, however, and her friend Pamela. The rest of the people attending the party were twelve Lebanese men. My shy enquiry as to who Samira was was met with hearty laughter at the confusion of the poor Dutchman. Luckily, André, a somewhat effeminate man with blond hair, was willing to enlighten me. Elie was known as 'Samira' to his friends, he told me. It was quite a common name with a somewhat coarse undertone, like the Dutch name 'Anita'. I found this hilarious. André himself is known as Saboeha, I also learned, which is the nickname of the Lebanese singer Sabah (later that evening he would perform as Saboeha).

André was a very talented singer. It turned out that he sang in church every Sunday. After this performance the presents were unwrapped. There was even one for me, in spite of the fact that I was a last-minute inclusion. Then, it was time to get active. We spent the rest of the night dancing merrily to Arabic music.

III Beirut Souks

Allow me to introduce you to Linda, one of my best friends. We used to work together and have taken wonderful trips to New York and Rio de Janeiro. That was before I fell in love with Lebanon. I had asked her many times to accompany me to this tiny Middle Eastern nation, and for a long time was unable to convince her. Linda's catastrophic love affair with a sweet-talking Muslim taxi driver had sworn her off any connection with the region, its inhabitants and its culture. But the stories I brought back from Lebanon slowly wore down her opposition and by the time she met Elie in Holland, she has crossed a milestone. If an open-minded man like Elie could come from Lebanon, surely it couldn't be so bad there. In fact, her attraction was growing to the country which was the background of all my stories, and her interest was particularly piqued by the friends and family of my dear friend Elie from Beirut. Moreover she learned that Lebanon is in fact anything but a – in her words – 'Muslim country'. Rather, it is a country full of churches, where alcohol is freely available and where there are gay bars, albeit not explicitly advertised.

We had been in Lebanon a few days when I offered to show Linda around in Beirut's centre. I did have an ulterior motive, but more about that later. The centre of the city is known among the locals by the Arabic term, *al balad* or, reflecting its French influence, *centre ville*. Potentially 'downtown' can be used in English, but not 'city centre', which will be met with a look of incomprehension from the locals. To complicate matters more, someone asking a taxi driver to go to *centre ville* may risk ending up in the similar-sounding district of Sin El Fil, which is miles away from the city centre. And I was once brought to a shopping mall called City Centre, which, ironically, is far from the actual centre of the city. In short, it's best to stick to *al balad*.

During the Civil War, as I explained to my friend Linda, the centre of Beirut was hit particularly hard. A demarcation line ran between the Christian East Beirut and Islamic West Beirut. It is called the 'green line' because nature took over after most people fled this border zone. The Jews of Lebanon were more affected than anybody else, because their quarter was in the centre. The green line tended to shift every now and again as a result of the ongoing battles. Of the severely damaged buildings and blackened corpses many of us saw on the TV news, much of the carnage took place in the centre of Beirut. It is there that the various factions, militias and foreign fighters bombarded one another. Anyone visiting the centre of Beirut should be aware of the horrific events that took place in that area during the war.

The Lebanese people have, however, done their best to obliterate their recent bloody past. Linda was quite astonished when we walked through downtown Beirut, knowing what had taken place there. Barely a week on, she had become quite used to the rather chaotic way of life in Beirut: whole sections of pavements were missing, anarchically-parked cars and litter everywhere. The city centre, in contrast, was far from chaotic; here the streets and pavements were spotless and there was no graffiti to be seen. Bollards prevented motorists from parking illegally, every single building looked brand new and instead of little bakeries and messy, overfull supermarkets, the streets were lined with pristine high-fashion shops offering all manner of luxury goods, such as Gucci and Louis Vuitton handbags and other upscale international brands. I explained to Linda that the street layout and buildings were exactly as they had been before the war. She nodded but was clearly still stunned to find Beirut so different to what she had expected. Only the heavy security around the government buildings and parliament reminded her of where she was. And yet, even in the city centre there are remarkable spots to visit, particularly ones that are of a religious nature such as the the Magen Avraham synagogue. The meticulous restoration of this synagogue was funded not only by Jewish individuals and organisations but also by the Solidare, the Sunni driven restoration company for the centre of Beirut. Even Hezbollah gave its blessing to the project, insisting that it respects 'divine religion' and has 'no problem with Jews, but with the State of Israel'.

To get to the synagogue you need to access the heavily guarded part of the city centre. I managed to go there only once. I simply asked the friendly soldier on duty if I could the see the synagogue. After scrutinising my identification papers, he pointed in the direction I should walk. He politely explained that I was only allowed to see the Jewish place of worship from the outside. Just a little while later, however, when I was casually leaning against the makeshift gate – the construction work was not yet fully completed – the door opened by itself. I looked behind me. The soldier had disappeared and I grabbed the chance to sneak inside. I couldn't help seeing this as a sign from above that I was allowed in.

The temple was soberly furnished and the colours were predominantly light blue with orange accents. It looked almost ready for use. Only the ark was missing, which, as in every other synagogue, would later hold the Torah scrolls and would only be opened during the Service. Struck by the overwhelming beauty of the building, I thought about the turbulent history it had witnessed, about an entire community that had become invisible. Till today, this beautiful synagogue has not been inaugurated. It's not completely clear why, but I assume that there is not much to gain for the Jewish community by using the place of worship again. It would expose the few Jewish families that are left, potentially making them a target for attacks. The question is whether the synagogue will ever be anything other than a beautiful museum piece.

Fortunately, other religious places of interest in the city centre are more welcoming to sightseers. And what tantalising sights they are! On the Place des Étoiles, in the heart of the city, is the Saint George Orthodox Cathedral. Easily accessible and for a little extra charge this splendid monument offers a small spectacle. In the church's vaults visitors are able to view the foundations dating back to Roman times. The huge mosque on Martyrs Square is also very much worth visiting. Male and female visitors are allowed to admire the Mohammed Al Amin mosque (also called the Rafiq Hariri mosque or Blue mosque) together. Adorned with enormous tapestries and gigantic chandeliers, I find this mosque to be one of the most beautiful Islamic places of worship I know, and I am not only referring to the interior of the building; the lighting of the four minarets is beautiful. At Christmastime the real party begins. An enormous Christmas tree is erected, complete with ornaments, and a huge crowd gathers around the tree, jostling to take selfies with the mosque and the tree in the background. From a few steps away, the photograph can even include the Maronite Cathedral behind of all of this.

I was there with Linda during her first visit to Lebanon. She was fascinated that even women wearing headscarves took selfies with their children at the Christmassy site. In her mixed neighbourhood in Amsterdam-West, home to many Muslims, she had never seen such a thing. I remember how Linda had used a selfie as a pretext to discreetly photograph a veiled woman in front of the Christmas tree.

But this time we hadn't come to *al balad* to see religious monuments. I wanted to introduce Linda to one of my oldest friends in Lebanon, a Palestinian man named Essam. Essam, who prefers to call himself Sam, is a gentle, friendly young man who loses his calm only when the conversation turns to Israel. I had met him during my first visit to Lebanon at the Christmas dinner of one of his friends. Sam was single and I saw no harm in introducing him to Linda, herself single at that time. It might turn out to be a good match, I thought. Sam was not only very intelligent but good-looking too. His light green eyes in particular stood out. Sam had chosen Beirut Souks as a meeting point. In most of Lebanon, the word *souq* has a romantic ring to it and usually refers to a kind of labyrinth of little stalls packed with handcrafted goods and fragrances from a thousand and one nights. Beirut Souks, however, is a shopping mall. Spotless, almost clinically clean and boasting all the famous brands. It's a place for Lebanese people to do what they do in any other enclosed shopping centre: shopping, socialising and flirting. We had barely entered the mall and stepped onto the escalator, when the clinical feel of it started to oppress Linda. 'Oh, how I miss the confusion and chaos of the rest of Beirut!' she sighed as we passed yet another cleaner frantically scrubbing to eliminate the slightest spot of dirt.

As I had expected, Sam hadn't yet arrived in the square where we had arranged to meet. We decided to sit down on a little bench opposite a sculpture consisting of man-sized letters reading 'I

LOVE BEIRUT' and wait. Fifteen minutes later Sam sent me a message: '*Habibi, sorry, problems with parking, please wait*'. Typical! How could he have expected parking to be easy in this overregulated city centre?

Another fifteen minutes later our patience was rewarded. There he was, but unfortunately not alone. With some annoyance, I recognised his companion. The most boring person you could imagine, very conservative and constantly talking about or quoting the Quran. I have had endless and pointless discussions with him, as he kept arguing that every word in the Quran was the word of God. This didn't stop him from dreaming of travelling to the Ukraine to see the beautiful women there. Sam excused him with a sly grin: 'He's a little backward, he's from the mountains.'

The four of us had a drink on the terrace of Dunkin' Donuts, a place where everything is made of plastic. In spite of my desperate efforts, it was quite a challenge to keep the conversation going. Whether this was caused by the company, Sam's tiresome friend or the fact that the pheromones were conspicuously absent: that essential spark between Sam and Linda failed to ignite. 'Nice man,' she remarked laconically. There was no point in elaborating.

IV Tofik wedding

Two years after I first met Elie I felt like he had always been a part of my life. Whenever I visited Lebanon I would stay at his house. We had become very close friends and spoke almost every day when I was in the Netherlands, and yet there were still things that puzzled me about him. I wondered, for example, how Elie, a 27 year-old assistant nurse with a modest salary and his partner Tofik, 41, a freelance translator who did not earn substantially either, had come to own such a vast top-floor apartment with a spacious terrace overlooking the whole city, as well as a studio apartment they had built themselves. I could not image that Elie's parents, who rented a simple two-room apartment, had helped Elie finance the purchase of the apartment, so I plucked up the courage to ask him point blank how they had got hold of the property. My question didn't surprise him in the least. 'Ah, didn't I tell you about Tofik wedding?' he asked simply. It was charming how Elie always made the same mistake in English by leaving out the "'s" to determine possession. He referred to my house as 'Martin house'. It turns out that many Arabic-speakers make this mistake in English, because in Arabic you would simply say '*beit* Martin' (house Martin).

'Er... wedding?' I echoed. To me, Elie and Tofik were a couple and I had never noticed Tofik show any interest in women. Besides, it was quite unclear to me what this apparent wedding had to do with the purchase of the apartment. From behind his laptop, Elie pursued his explanation through the sounds of Bourj Hammoud that I was gradually getting used to: cars tooting and accelerating, souped-up mopeds, loud church bells and the murmur of a far-away call to prayer.

When he and Tofik became involved with one another ten years before, there had been a sense of foreboding that sooner or later confronts any Lebanese man who has not shown an interest in marriage. It starts with continuous pressure from his parents, who point out that their son has reached the appropriate age and has a duty to search for a wife. If he shows no willingness, they will look for a suitable partner themselves. When Tofik became aware it was his time, he started looking for a girl who might benefit from a fake marriage as well. Being a Druze, this was even more complicated, because he was allowed only to marry a woman from his tribe.

The Druze are known in the Middle East as being tough people. You do not mess with the Druze, especially when it comes to family affairs. Let me illustrate this with an example. Rabih Ahmad, fell deeply in love with Ruydayna Melaab, a Druze girl. He was 39 years old and she only 19. They met on Facebook and their liaison grew into genuine love. Rabih, a Sunni Muslim, decided to pose as a Druze in order to be granted permission to marry his beloved. The marriage was performed without Ruydayna's family. It was in actual fact a Sunni ceremony (as civil weddings do not exist in Lebanon). Unsurprisingly, the secret was discovered to the fury of the girl's family. Initially the two families appeared willing to settle the issue. Rabih was invited by the Melaab family to discuss the issue in their village of Baysour. Instead of smelling a rat, Rabih took the fatal decision to accept the invitation. Upon his arrival he was brutally beaten by the bride's father and brother on the local village square. They pulled out some of his teeth, battered his testicles and then, worst of all, sliced off his penis. I remember that terrible event very well. It happened in the summer of 2013 and everyone was talking about it in Lebanon at the time. It was a clear message that anyone who dared to defy the Druze would pay for it dearly.

Like the unfortunate Rabih, Tofik met his lover online. Unluckily, not only did Elie practise the wrong religion, he also had the wrong sex. Finding a Druze bride or bridegroom for a fake marriage however was difficult, as this tribe makes up only five percent of the Lebanese population. But Elie and Tofik hit the jackpot when they found a Druze lesbian among the gay community of Beirut who was willing to pose as Tofik's bride. The parents of the newlyweds were naturally overjoyed. The couple was duly engaged and married. No trouble or expense was spared for the wedding. In total, 20 000 dollars were spent on the location, drinks and masses of food. In Lebanon spending such an amount of money on a wedding is by no means out of the ordinary, as not only close family and friends are invited, but also friends of friends and distant family members. The number of wedding guests may total up to five hundred or more. Elie, in his role as Tofik's best man, found the charade appalling. Not being able to be himself was unbearable to him. During the party he could hardly resist the temptation to kiss Tofik right on the mouth but common sense prevailed. The wedding night, or rather the run-up to it, formed the final act of this performance. The wedding couple left for a hotel by taxi. But unbeknownst to the waving crowd, further down the road another taxi waited with Elie and the bride's girlfriend in the backseat. The four of them met at a pre-arranged place where the exchange took place. 'You should have seen the reaction of the taxi drivers. They had never seen anything like it!' Elie chuckled. 'I quickly ducked into Tofik taxi while the bride ran in her long wedding dress to the cab in which her girlfriend was waiting.'

And so Elie, Tofik and the lesbian couple eventually arrived in the apartment where they all lived. Tofik's parents paid a large part of the deposit for the purchase of the apartment as a wedding gift. The rest was borrowed from a bank. Sharing the apartment with the lesbian couple eventually turned out to be problematic. Tofik's marriage was annulled to the great sadness of his parents and the two women moved out soon afterwards. The two rooms that became available were advertised on Airbnb as 'rooms in a straight friendly house'. In an ironic twist of fate, Tofik's parents, with their traditional religious values, had enabled Elie and Tofik to set up a safe haven for gays in Beirut.

V Venturing into Shatila

'Mafia, mafia!!!' the cabdriver muttered, shaking his head at my German-Palestinian companion, Nino, and me when we asked him to drive us to the Palestinian camp of Shatila. His reaction didn't ease the apprehension we already had about visiting this part of Beirut, known to be a hotbed of crime. Terrorist organisations such as Al Nusra and ISIS allegedly recruit from Palestinian camps. And then there is the inescapable past: the Sabra and Shatila massacres of 1982, when thousands of Palestinians and Shiite Muslims were slaughtered in cold blood as a reprisal for the murder of Christian President Bashir Gemayel. For three days, members of the Christian militia, Phalange, one of the most ruthless in the Civil War, went on the rampage, backed by Israeli army units who sealed off the camp, thus enabling the militiamen to kill, maim and rape without constraint. The Israeli occupation forces even illuminated the sky at night to help the Phalangists.

The Sabra and Shatila bloodbaths represent one of the darkest pages in Lebanon's history. To add to the horror of the whole event, it later emerged that the Palestinians had had no hand in the killing of the President: on the exact day that the Phalangists invaded the camp, the Christian Lebanese Habib Shartouni was arrested for the murder of Gemayel. Shartouni confessed to the assassination and managed to escape after eight years, without being convicted, to Syria, which itself was suspected of being behind the attack.

The taxi left us just outside Shatila, in front of the Rafiq Hariri II school. This exceptionally well-maintained building with its newly whitewashed walls was in the care of a friendly guard named Mohammed. Grateful to break the monotony of his day, Mohammed chatted to us about Dutch football (he especially liked Van Persie), Dutch weather ('Always rain!') and Amsterdam ('Can you really smoke cannabis there?!'). While we waited for our Palestinian friend Sam who (of course) was delayed, Mohammed insisted on 'friending' us on Facebook. He recently sent me a message asking if I knew any nice single women who might be looking for a husband – I promised him I would think about it.

My very first meeting with Sam is still clear in my mind. It was at a Christmas party in 2013 and he was sitting on a couch, enjoying a snack, when he introduced himself to me. The fact that he was a Palestinian intrigued me as I had never met one before. I soon realised that I was in conversation with an extremely intelligent young man. Sam owned an internet café alongside his job in the IT department of a multinational firm. When he told me that he lived in Shatila, I couldn't believe my luck: would he be prepared to show me around if he could spare the time? His first reaction was one of disbelief. 'Why would you want to see Shatila? It's filthy and dangerous', he replied. I had already explained that I was a journalist and was thus drawn to the parts of Beirut that fell outside the regular tourist path.

And so it came about that on a beautiful spring day, Elie's German tenant Nino and I set off to discover Shatila. We entered the area through a gate adorned with a face of Yasser Arafat –

the first of many portraits of the Palestinian leader throughout the camp. I was struck by the fact that Shatila didn't look like a typical refugee camp. Instead of tents, concrete blocks had been erected, very close together. Some of these were in a terrible state, with missing windows, and sometimes unfinished, without even a roof. The five- or six-storey buildings with no lifts were separated by narrow alleyways that were swarming with children of all ages. The overcrowded place made me claustrophobic and I was grateful when Sam suggested we visit the UNRWA building. UNRWA is a United Nations agency which provides assistance and protection to Palestinian refugees. Its well-maintained office, situated on a small square, stood out among the dilapidated buildings surrounding it. Inside, there was no child in sight due to the school holidays, and I felt able to breathe again.

To my disappointment, there wasn't anything remarkable to see in the office building and the lady on duty did not share any captivating stories with us. Sam had explained that the UNRWA building functioned as a kind of community centre where information was disseminated and skills training for adults was offered. UNRWA provides Shatila residents with badly needed healthcare, education, social services and relief from their daily struggle. It certainly is not an undue luxury in a place that is inhabited not only by many Palestinians, but also several thousand poor Syrians, Sudanese, Iraqis and Yeminis. In practice, Shatila serves as a last resort home for people who cannot afford to live in the ordinary poor districts of the city. The actual number of residents is unknown. According to UNWRA there are 10 000 registered Palestinian refugees but the continuing influx of migrants make the real – much higher – figure impossible to determine.

A recent survey found that the number of Palestinian refugees in Lebanon as a whole is much lower than previously thought. While around 500 000 refugees from Palestine are registered at UNWRA, the 2017 census held among Palestinians counted 175 000 people. Many fled abroad to escape the unenviable status they had in Lebanon: Palestinians have no voting rights or access to regular healthcare and are banned from twenty-two professions, including the practice of politics, law and medicine. Lebanese citizenship can be obtained by means of marriage, but this is only possible for Palestinian women – for Palestinian men, regretfully, the motto 'once a Palestinian, always a Palestinian' applies. Because of this, Sam's rancour is not only with Israel, but with the Lebanese government as well. His dream is to leave Lebanon, but which country is willing to give a residence permit to a stateless Palestinian man from Lebanon? Even an application for a tourist visa to visit his family in Sweden was rejected.

After the peace and quiet of the UN building, Sam took us to a much less tranquil location: the notorious local street market. Here you will find any product that cannot be purchased on the regular market, and this partly explains why Lebanese police do not venture into Palestinian refugee camps. Sam would not allow us to explore the full length of the market. 'Too dangerous', he declared, but I was unconvinced. Was there something he didn't want me to see? I was hardly going to be scandalised by pornographic DVDs or handguns on display. I believe it was more to do with preserving his own image: this was his neighbourhood and he wanted me to remember its better sides.

Sam's internet café was located off one of the many alleyways. To his surprise, the blinds of his little shop were closed. Grumbling that his staff was irresponsible and untrustworthy, he took a bunch of keys out of his pocket, inserted one into the lock and the blinds flew open. The café contained four computers with old-fashioned monitors, the kind with 22 inches of depth behind the screen. For a while he had sold beer in his shop, but that had got him into trouble: threats from conservative Muslims in the camp made him decide to stick to soft drinks. Devoid of customers, the little café could not give us an idea of how successful it normally was, but I was immensely impressed by Sam's entrepreneurship and congratulated him. My compliment was in earnest: Sam worked extremely hard to make ends meet, that at least was obvious.

Although we had planned to leave Shatila before sunset, it was already getting dark when we reached the apartment block where Sam lived. The stairwell didn't have even the faintest trace of lighting, so guided by the flashlight on his iphone Sam led us up the stairs to where his widower father was waiting to meet us. We were introduced to a cheerful man of around sixty, with bright eyes twinkling in his deeply tanned face. Two of Sam's brothers, one of whom had the most beautiful green eyes I had ever seen, joined us in the living room. It was an all-male gathering – completely normal in traditional Islamic families. I did not see nor was ever introduced to my friend's sisters.

The living area was surprisingly spacious and well looked-after. Except for a few framed texts from the Quran, the walls were bare. As far as the furniture was concerned, however, no effort had been spared. We sat down on a splendidly comfortable and probably expensive sofa bedecked with lush cushions. The television was tuned to an Arabic news channel and they even had Wi-Fi. Sam's family was clearly not among the neediest.

Excusing himself, supposedly to the kitchen to fetch us tea, Sam's father only reappeared after a long while. Immediately it was clear why it had taken so long. In his arms was a large box full of Arab delicacies. While Sam's younger brother – the one with the striking green eyes – poured the tea, baklava and other fancy pastries were set out on the table. Sam's father watched with delight as we indulged. 'Good, good. Eat please', he urged.

Nino and I were then treated to an account of Sam's family history. Although of Turkish descent, Sam's father was born in Haifa (present day Israel) a fact of which he was visibly proud. His greatest wish was to travel once again to Haifa to the house he had left behind. I asked him about his departure from Palestine. Instead of condemning the Israelis as I had expected, the sixty year-old told us how the Arabs had betrayed their Palestinian brothers. In 1947, they had been asked to leave their homes with the promise that they would be welcomed back as soon as the war was over. They complied with the request, not anticipating that the Arab nations of Egypt, Jordan, Syria and Iraq would lose their fight against the Jewish army. The subsequent closing of the borders meant that Sam's family, like so many Palestinians, were forced to remain in Lebanon. Other Palestinian families during that war, often called *al-Nakba* (the catastrophe), were driven off their land, often by force. I already knew about *al-Nakba* but the part about Palestinians being betrayed by the Arab nations was new to me.

I didn't question that Sam's father's account was accurate. Why would he lie? People like him had no sympathy for Israel whatsoever. Researching the matter, I found that the cause of the Palestinian exodus is the subject of heated debate. According to estimates by the Israeli author Benny Morris, at least five percent of the Palestinians fled their land following calls by Arab leaders to do so. Arab sources authenticate that there was pressure from that corner: both the Syrian Prime Minister at the time, Khalid Al-Azm, and the Palestinian UN representative, Jamal Husseini, have confirmed the fact.

Unexpectedly, twenty-four year old Nino, whom I had only known for a few days, was inspired to share his own remarkable story. I learned, to my surprise, that his father had been Palestinian, originally from southern Lebanon, but had died shortly after Nino was born, leaving the child to be raised by his German mother. Nino had moved to Beirut to study Arabic and International Relations, not to uncover his family history. But once there, he felt an increasing yearning to learn more about his Palestinian kin. He started with practically no knowledge about his father's relatives; neither in which refugee camp they might be or even whether they were still alive. Knowing only that his father was from the south, he began his search in the notoriously dangerous Lebanese camp, Ain al-Hilweh, near the city of Saida (Sidon). Armed with just a photograph, he asked people at random whether they had known his father. Incredibly, he did find his family. They welcomed Nino with open arms and invited him to stay with them for a week. From that moment onwards he felt a great deal less German and, for the first time in his life, more Palestinian. It was one of the most beautiful experiences of his life, he told us, as we listened with bated breath to his moving story.

One of Sam's younger brothers who seemed to have a good grasp of English beckoned us over to a bedroom that overlooked the street. One of the windows had been transformed into a kind of spider web. In the middle of the glass pane was a hole surrounded by concentric circles of cracked glass. The young boy pointed to the ground where the bullet responsible for the hole still lay. Our German friend went pale and dart straight back to the other room. Ever practical, Sam simply said that the family would not be sleeping in the street-side rooms for the time being. He added reassuringly that this was the first time that his father's house had been hit at and that it was probably a stray bullet rather than a targeted attack. Nevertheless, we found at our next visit that the family had moved to a location just outside the camp.

It was about ten o'clock when we finally said goodbye to Sam's father, thanked him for his hospitality and left Shatila. Sam escorted us back through the pitch darkness of the camp to the place our day's adventure had begun, the Rafiq Hariri school. Mohammed – whom I met again years later in front of Beirut's Four Seasons hotel – was still at his post. After a short exchange we settled into the waiting taxi. During the drive home Nino and I didn't say very much. I'm sure that he, like me, was wrestling with mixed feelings from the afternoon's events. We were heading to a comparatively safe environment. The kind family we were leaving behind was reasonably well off, but most people in Shatila weren't. It was a dismal place.

VI The House Of Khalil Gibran

What Rembrandt is to the Dutch, Khalil Gibran is to the people of Lebanon. The most acclaimed author the nation has produced, Gibran's most famous book, *The Prophet,* still holds bestseller status in his native country. Since it was first published in 1923, millions of copies have been printed of the book. The author takes his place next to Shakespeare as most popular poet of all time. In 2014 *The Prophet* was turned into an animated film produced by Salma Hayek, for which she also did the voiceover. In preparation for her role in the film, Hayek spent a week in the village where Gibran was born.

Gibran grew up in abject poverty and, in lieu of school, attended bible and grammar lessons provided by the village clerics. His life and work depict a Lebanon of the past as well as the present. Like millions of other Lebanese people, Gibran's family emigrated in order to escape the devastating hardship in their country. The dream of leaving is still in the hearts of many young Lebanese today, in spite of their love for their homeland which simply has nothing to offer them. Added to the bleak economic situation is the constant threat of terrorism and war. In Gibran's time the situation was not very different, marked as it was by frequent infighting between religious groups. In those days Lebanon did not exist. The much smaller Mount Lebanon belonged to the Ottoman Empire but had achieved (with great difficulty) a semi-autonomous status. The Maronites, a Christian community that acknowledges the position of the pope, regularly clashed with the Islamic population of the Turkish Empire. Gibran's work reveals his exposure from a young age to different religions. His mystic works, including *The Prophet*, are clearly inspired by Christianity, but also contain elements borrowed from Islam, Sufism (a spiritual movement within Islam) and Judaism. In this sense, the poet was typically Lebanese, Lebanon being, as it was in the early nineteenth century, a kind of crossroads of the three major monotheistic religions. In addition, the Buddhist and Bahá'í faiths and theosophy he encountered while living in New York, appear in his writings.

Another typically Lebanese aspect of Gibran's life is that, although he emigrated to the United States at a relatively young age (he was 12 years old), Gibran's heart remained in his beloved country and indeed he returned to study in Lebanon shortly afterwards. The museum that holds his remains has clearly influenced Graceland, the home of one of his admirers, Elvis Presley. The latter is not alone among music icons in his fascination with the poet: John Lennon and Johnny Cash are said to have been inspired by Gibran's writings. Every day, literary pilgrims flock to the village of Bsharri where he spent his childhood.

To be completely honest, I had never actually heard of the renowned Lebanese writer when Elie offered to take me to visit his birthplace. But I didn't pass up the opportunity when I found out that it was just a short drive from the famous Cedar Forest, which I was eager to see.

Phoenicians in the Old Testament built their ships from cedar wood and this gigantic tree is honoured as national symbol on the Lebanese flag. Large parts of Lebanon were once covered with cedar forests, but due to the high demand for this extraordinarily strong wood, only two parts of Lebanon remain where cedar forests can be found: near Bsharri and in the Chouf mountains in central Lebanon.

Our plan was originally to take the first bus from Beirut to Bsharri in the early hours of the morning. An early start is unpleasant at the best of times, but being on holiday we were even more keen to avoid it. So we counted ourselves very lucky when Elie managed to whet Rabih's appetite for a visit to the cedar forest. A young student and the son of a well-to-do Lebanese family, Rabih had studied in Paris, travelled throughout Europe but, to my astonishment, had never visited the cedar forest or Gibran's birthplace. He agreed that it was about time he did. And so it happened that on a bright summer's morning in 2013, the three of us drove at high speed towards the forest. Rabih turned out to be a very skilled – and very fast – driver. His technique for taking turns was to accelerate, brake slightly just before the bend and then hit maximum speed around corners. It proved to be too nerve-racking for my Dutch friend, Stijn, who was joining us on this trip. I, on the other hand, found Rabih's confidence reassuring: if he could drive at such a high speed along ravines without any fear, surely he knew what he was doing. Then, suddenly we stopped right beside a steep precipice. I thought there must be something wrong with the car, but Rabih rolled down his window and pointed to a village glistening in the distance, the church with its red dome and two spires, prominent. 'That's where we are going', he said with emotion. There, nestled in the Kadisha Valley, was Bsharri.

I pictured Gibran travelling down this same mountain road to Beirut, with his mother, brother and sister, to catch the boat to New York, and of the prophet Almustafa in Gibran's famous book announcing his departure to his followers, after twelve years in their midst. Twelve years! Exactly the age of little Khalil at the start of his new life in the United States, and also the number of years later that he wrote his masterpiece in America. The book does not lack symbolism; the inhabitants of Orphalese have a final opportunity to put questions to their prophet before he leaves them for good. Their first question is about love; the last is about death. *The Prophet* is described as a spiritual self-help book that is before its time, in which Gibran shares his spiritual insights with his readers in a way that it makes them accessible.

Gibran's house itself did not enthral me: an ordinary stone house with a bare floor, and a scattering of wooden furniture. The impression you leave with is a sense of the utter destitution the family must have experienced, which is unsurprising given that Gibran's father gambled away the little money he earned. He took up employment as a tax collector for the Ottoman Empire but the lethal combination of being a gambler and a tax collector came to a catastrophic conclusion when he was arrested for committing fraud. His house was confiscated and his wife and children ended up on the street. Gibran's mother, Kamileh, saw no other option than to follow her brother who had already settled in the United States.

Gibran's desire to be buried in Lebanon after his death says something about his love for his birth country. In 1926 he and his sister bought a Carmelite monastery where he intended to spend the last days of his life. Part of the purchase was a cave, which seventh-century Christians used to hide from Muslim persecution. Upon his death in 1931, the poet's body was laid to rest in that cave, just as he had wished. The tomb is the last step of the museum tour, which runs past books, notes and hundreds of Gibran's paintings (of which there are 440 in the museum).

Although the house and the museum didn't leave a lasting impression on me, unlike the spectacular surroundings, I could not resist buying Gibran's famous *The Prophet* from the museum shop. An unremarkable little book of just a hundred and twenty-five pages including an introduction detailing the author's life – I wasn't immediately mesmerised. Not until I delved into it the next day, on the sunny balcony in Bourj Hammoud, when the melodic verses, rhythm and mysticism captivated me. Poetry that was also prose. A message to the world that slowly resonated in my soul; Gibran's words are shrouded in mysticism. The ending, a thought about death that embodies hope, a Druze notion: 'A little while, a moment of rest upon the wind, and another woman shall bear me.'

VII Magical food

'*Hayete*, I have been so sick the last few days', André sighed after we climbed into his comfortable Chevrolet. He had inherited the car from his brother who had passed away far too young. 'I won't be able to sing for you tonight', André said, his voice was hoarse and his expression pained. '*Akid*, it is really great that you are joining us for dinner', I said from the back seat. 'But of course *hayete*. It is your last day in Beirut. Your Beirut, your city!' As he pronounced the word *hayete* (meaning 'my life'), André held up his right hand, as he always did, forefinger outstretched and tracing circles in front of his face.

Tofik was also in the car, along with Paul, the twenty-four year old fashion designer who had been deaf from birth and Turina, a German student who was renting a room in Tofik's house. With directions provided by Elie André was trying to find the Armenian restaurant where we had decided to have dinner. According to him there was no better place to eat Armenian food in Lebanon.

As the rain gushed down on André's Chevrolet, we entered Bourj Hammoud, the Armenian neighbourhood which I now knew well. As ever, Elie's instructions were confusing: should we take a left by the bridge towards Mar Mikhael, or rather to turn into another street off the main road? Sitting in the front seat, Tofik kept up a constant exchange on Whatsapp with Elie, passing the directions on to André as well as he could. Meanwhile, in the back seat, Paul and I had our own scribbled 'conversation' on a notepad. He wanted to know exactly what the others were saying. 'Nothing,' I assured him, 'Tofik is just trying to find the restaurant with Elie's help.'

Too late, we realised that we should have taken the left turn before the bridge and André turned the car around. As it happens so often in Lebanon, the street lights were not working and all I could see was a pit of darkness for us to drive into. Almost immediately, André stopped the car on Tofik's orders and we all stepped out onto the curb, letting André try to find a parking space (no easy task in this neighbourhood with its narrow, one-way streets and over-full car parks.

We were standing in front of a corner house with light shining through the windows. Above our heads on the second-floor, intricate oriel windows protruded from the salmon-hued building. Through one of the ground floor windows I glimpsed a large empty room with carefully set tables. There was nobody in sight. 'I don't know if they're even open', Tofik remarked as we walked towards the side entrance. I pushed against the imposing wooden door but to no avail. There was something eerie about the situation: an empty restaurant, with the tables set and the dining area brightly lit, but seemingly closed.

Turina rang the bell. Just as I had given up hope that anybody would answer, a strikingly beautiful young woman appeared in the doorway. Her hair was long and dark, her clothes somewhat old-fashioned and she exuded an almost superhuman aura of calm. 'Is the restaurant open?' I asked in English. She nodded and beckoned us to follow after what seemed like too long a pause. We walked behind her down a corridor, turned around a corner to the left and found ourselves in the empty dining area we had seen from the outside. When I looked around, the young woman had vanished. I wondered simultaneously how she could have escaped my attention so suddenly – and why she had not led us to a table as normally happens in a restaurant.

We chose a long, neatly-laid table at the far end of the room. From the number of prepared tables, it looked like the restaurant was fully booked that evening. White plates rested on red paper place-mats that featured the name of the restaurant, *Badguèr*, in large letters. Our table was covered with a lace tablecloth. The light in the room was just a little too bright for comfort. I had never visited Armenia but imagined that the canteens in that country were similar to this room.

We had been waiting for at least ten minutes when the myste-rious Armenian woman reappeared at our table. She seemed to materialise out of nothing, like a kind of spirit that could move about the room unseen. She handed each of us a wooden board with the menu attached to it. Although Tofik had eaten here before with Elie, he was as much at a loss as the rest of us when it came to decrypting the menu and eventually he requested a 'mix of typical Armenian dishes'. In response the young woman listed some of the most popular options, of which I only recog-nised batata hara: chunks of spicy baked potato. Tofik, as much in the dark as I was, opted to leave the selection entirely up to our host.

While we waited for our food I wandered around the dining room which was still empty. A sideboard behind our table carried two framed black and white photos. Above it on the wall was a family portrait. All of the people in the photograph looked very serious. It must have been taken at a solemn occasion. Judging by the clothing, I guessed the photo was taken at the beginning of the twentieth century, at the time of the Armenian genocide by the Turks. Armenians had fled to the furthermost corners of the Ottoman Empire, including Lebanon, to escape persecution. I wondered if the people on the photographs had succumbed to the mass slaughter. For a moment I actually sensed their presence in the room, as if we were no longer alone. Tofik saw me staring at the photos and seemed to read my mind. 'It feels like great injustice has been done to these people'. he said. 'I feel as if they are here now', I replied. Tofik nodded. His Druze faith upheld the notions of spirits and reincarnation. Paul wanted to know what Tofik and I were talking about, but I found it very hard to find the words. I wrote: 'We discussed if these pictures are family pictures.' He looked disbelieving at me.

By the time our food arrived, more diners had filled the empty seats. It appeared that this restaurant also functioned as a kind of heritage centre. I heard people speaking English behind me, as a group of four twenty-something year-olds argued about what to order. The Armenian waiter arrived with a tray full of tasty nibbles. Olives, hummus and bread were set before us along with spicy lamb meatballs something similar to nachos which we dipped into a hot red sauce. The sauce, especially, was out of this world, and the food disappeared in no time. There was more to come. For me the highlight was a crispy pasta-type dish topped with both a yoghurt sauce and a spicy dark green dressing. The acidity of one competed with the fieryness of the other on my taste buds while the pasta soothed, balanced and unified the whole experience. It is difficult to describe the overall effect. The particular blend of spices reminded me vaguely of Indian cooking, which is not surprising given Armenia's place on the centuries-old trade route to India. The batata hara, the seasoned potatoes, were particularly spicy, even by Lebanese standards. With the exception of André, who was not only sick but also not keen on spicy food, everyone spoke fervently about the meal. I wrote in Paul's notebook: 'The food is magic.' In response he just pushed the book back to me and nodded. Verbal confirmation was unnecessary.

When we had finished, the table next to us had already emptied, as if the two English couples had never been there. Had I just imagined them? The food had been so delectable that I had been oblivious to everything around us. As we walked through the brightly lit room towards the hall, we noticed for the first time an elderly Armenian lady sitting in the corner. How long had she been there? Well into her seventies, she looked fragile with her grey hair pulled into a bun and a long dress decorated with dark flowers. She smiled kindly at us from behind her table. We enthusiastically expressed our appreciation of the food and she seemed to know enough English to understand. We later found out from Elie that the delicacies put before us were her creations. She possessed that same serene energy as the Armenian woman who had served us earlier. The latter led us to the exit, wished us a good night and locked the door behind us. André pulled up in his car and I waited for the lights to fade in *Badguèr*. I wasn't sure I agreed with Tofik that the restaurant was haunted. What I did know for a fact, was that the food was magic.

VIII Recycle Beirut

In Lebanon you won't find any bio or glass containers and much less a deposit and return system for plastic bottles. Everything is thrown into the dustbin without hesitation. Most people put their rubbish out on the curb, except in affluent areas, where that task is left to the concierge. Before the lorries have a chance to collect the rubbish, Syrians with pushcarts are often quicker off the mark. They transport the refuse to one of the many sorting locations in the city where plastic, cardboard and metal items that can be sold on the market are filtered out.

One of these sorting stations was near where I was living; a dilapidated shed on an abandoned urban grass field. Either the owner of the land lived abroad or whoever had inherited the property didn't consider it worth exploiting. From a good distance already, the smell of waste was intense. Under the midday sun I noticed young men digging through the waste. Some of them had gloves, but most used their bare hands. For a pittance, they did a job that most Lebanese people would never even contemplate. I always tried to walk past these places as inconspicuously as possible. Not out of fear, but out of shame. There was I, on my way to a restaurant or an excursion while those poor men spent their day rooting through somebody else's waste. What future was there for them?

In the summer of 2015 the stench of rubbish dumps overpowered the whole city. In spite of the warnings I had received prior to my trip, I was completely unprepared for the sheer extent of the crisis. I had barely stepped into the car on my way from the airport to Elie and Tofik's house when I clearly detected the smell of sewage and then saw the huge heaps of waste along the roadside. Sukleen (nicknamed 'not so clean' by locals even before the 2015 crisis) was the company responsible for collecting Beirut's waste, and in July of that year, it simply stopped its work as the collection sites had reached the point of overflowing. That was three weeks before my arrival. The many Bangladeshi dustmen – (you won't see Lebanese men in this line of work) – sat at home twiddling their thumbs. It was not unexpected that the waste collection sites might one day be full but those in charge had ignored the signs and continuously postponed taking any action.

Even through the twelfth floor window of my building I was occasionally assailed by the stink. People from the neighbourhood were resorting to setting fire to the rubbish heaps in order to stop the spread of disease and to reduce the stench. This in turn filled the air with toxic smoke. I would watch these fires from my balcony with amazement. For the first time, I was happy that this was only a four-day visit to Beirut.

Local outrage against the authorities was already palpable when I was there and would later lead to mass protests in the city. It did nothing to improve the public's already low esteem of the country's politicians. According to my friends, the latest developments proved that the political elite was corrupt and didn't care at all about the people's struggles. Politicians had a vested interest in Sukleen, they said, it represented a great deal of money. A foreign company would probably collect the waste at a far cheaper rate. I wondered why they didn't ship the excessive waste over to Europe. It seemed to be a lucrative business.

'Waste is a gold mine! Think of all the cardboard, plastic, metal, glass you can recover', affirmed my Palestinian friend Sam, while gratefully accepting my gift of Dutch treacle waffles. 'But Lebanese people would rather die of hunger than retrieve this gold. Collecting waste is beneath them', he continued. Sam had good news to tell me: he and an American acquaintance called Alex had founded Recycle Beirut, a company that collects, sorts and makes arrangements for the recycling of waste. Their aim was to carry out this task far more professionally than the Syrian waste sorters, he explained. Alex and he would approach organisations, such as embassies and big companies and offer them an exclusive contract. Recycle Beirut would collect their rubbish and would ensure it is recycled. This was an attractive prospect for non-governmental organisations and Western-based corporations. Sam was in the process of identifying suitable storage for the waste, machines to process the paper and plastic and workers to employ. I admired how enterprising he was, particularly considering that he already had a fulltime job.

Two months later the waste had completely disappeared. On my next visit the streets of Beirut were spotless, at least compared with before. 'Where has the rubbish gone?' I asked. This made my Lebanese friends laugh. 'Pure magic!' someone replied. 'The same trick they use to make money disappear has been used on the rubbish', another friend chuckled, referring to the local government's corrupt reputation. Another friend was more resigned: 'It has just been dumped somewhere else where fewer people are burdened with it.' Indeed, it seemed that the politicians had been unable to come to an agreement on this issue. There were rumours that the waste mountain had been sold to Sierra

Leone and was rotting away there, but according to sources in the Lebanese media, it had been left somewhere just outside Beirut. Aerial photos later confirmed the latter to be the case. It didn't matter to most people in Beirut anyway. They were glad to be rid of the stench and smoke and that the risk of diseases like cholera had now been averted. As for me, I could put away the pollution masks I had brought with me – the kind I often see worn by Japanese tourists in Amsterdam.

I had planned to visit Sam's recycling company in the southern part of Beirut. But as usual, there was confusion as to the location where we were supposed to meet. When the taxi dropped me right on time at the address Sam had indicated – by the shopping mall called Mall of America, where the office was supposedly located – the mall itself was nowhere in sight. Sam was not answering his mobile phone or replying to my WhatsApp messages. Remembering that Sam had mentioned that his depot was located in an old, abandoned car park put me on the right track. Twenty metres further up the road was an entrance that looked out of use and, just as I approached it, Sam came towards me with his American associate Alex, an energetic thirty year-old who had fallen in love with Lebanon. Together we walked down to what had once been the car park for visitors to the shopping mall. One floor up, where the shopping paradise used to be, Syrian refugees had made their home. On the ground floor were small businesses, such as Recycle Beirut. We were assailed at the entrance by a smell of urine. Evidently, this was where the toilets were located. I didn't glance inside but could imagine the dreadful state they must have been in. I could tell from outside that the lights were broken.

The first thing that I noticed when we entered the depot was a yellowish-green machine you would expect to find in a factory. It was made of metal, about the height of a man and looked extremely heavy. It was still wrapped in plastic. 'Just delivered from China', Sam said proudly. 'It compresses the cardboard'. A very tall man joined us and was introduced by Sam as the warehouse manager. We walked past piles of plastic and cardboard. The smell here was much more bearable as there was no organic waste. Sam wanted to introduce me to one more person, a somewhat older, corpulent man who emerged from behind a pile of cardboard. He seemed to be the only person here who got his hands dirty. He was somewhat taken aback when I reached out to shake his hand.

Because Alex's command of the Arabic language was still shaky, most of the communication took place in English and as a result, I learned a lot in a fairly short time. Among other things, I discovered that the company had not yet earned a single penny; that the men who collected the rubbish for Recycle Beirut were still waiting, at that stage, for their wages (they did get paid later). First, the yellowish-green machine needed to be set up and start working. For this, electricity was needed which, in Beirut, was available only erratically and not always with enough voltage for this huge machine. An alternative would be to install a diesel generator but that plan was met with opposition by the warehouse manager (what a job title!), who never seemed to be in agreement with Sam and Alex.

Later that day we shared a meal in a restaurant in Verdun, a neighbourhood as chic as the name suggests. The Italian owner had clearly moved with the times, employing an army of Japanese chefs to make sushi. The sushi was prepared in front of us and laid on a kind of assembly line. The majority of the diners were wealthy Lebanese couples, stylishly dressed in designer outfits. We decided to stick with a delicious, old-fashioned pizza that nevertheless cost at least twice as much as it would have in our 'shabby' Bourj Hammoud. Suddenly, the absurdity of the situation struck me. Alex and Sam were virtually penniless. Their workers had not yet been paid. They could not afford diesel for the generator. And here we were having an expensive meal in an exclusive restaurant. Thank goodness for credit cards! Alex paid the bill, without guilt but with an awkward smile. I put my share on the table.

Bucra is the Arabic equivalent of the Spanish word *mañana*, and is often used in the songs of Fairuz. Live in the moment; *bucra* (tomorrow) we will solve our problems. That's the way it goes in Lebanon.

Recycle Beirut still exists and has become bigger and better over the years. The non-profit organisation counts many embassies and non-governmental organisations among its clientele.

IX Hezbollah

Anyone who flies into Lebanon and lands at Rafiq Hariri Airport indirectly and unknowingly comes into contact with Hezbollah. It is this militant group that carefully monitors from behind the scenes every movement that takes place in and around the airport, using their own security staff. Although this may sound alarming, the result is that the airport has become a kind of safe oasis. None of the bombs that have exploded in Lebanon in the past years has struck the airport. There were no hijackings or bombs on board any flights since the Civil War. But rumours persist about the lack of safety at Rafiq Hariri airport and it is worth taking a minute to consider who might stand to gain from these. Opponents of the Iranian-backed Hezbollah recognise that the fact that the airport is controlled by an armed militia does nothing to attract visitors to Lebanon.

In 2008, the Lebanese government made an unsuccessful attempt to put an end to this situation, by trying to dismantle Hezbollah's internal military communication network at the airport. This sparked an armed response by Hezbollah against Lebanese security forces, which caused a number of deaths and led to the closure by Hezbollah of the roads that provide access to the airport.

Then, there was the kidnapping of two Turkish Airlines pilots in August 2013, right under the noses of Lebanese security staff. Although Hezbollah denies involvement in the latter scenario, there were definitely political motives behind the abduction. This is underpinned by the fact that the pilots' release coincided with that of a number of Shiite pilgrims who had been held hostage in Syria. Also, Turkey, who acted as a mediator in this deal, happens to be keen to unseat Hezbollah's close friend, Syrian President Al Assad. It is tempting to conclude that the pilots were freed in exchange for Shiite pilgrims, but this is speculation.

While tourists may not be able to avoid the airport, they can easily stay away from the other Hezbollah bastion, the city of Baalbek, which lies somewhat isolated in the east, close to the Syrian border. Before the civil war in Syria, Baalbek constituted one of the main tourist attractions in Lebanon. For years, the ancient ruins of this Roman acropolis drew hordes of visitors and the Baalbeck International Music Festival, held every summer in the Beqaa Valley, made it a busy time of the year for the country's tourist industry.

When the Syrian war broke out, all of this changed. The Baalbek area was hit repeatedly by rockets and there was a real fear of insurgents crossing the border. However, Hezbollah has cleared the Syrian side of rebels and their presence in Arsal, a Lebanese city north of Baalbek, also ended in 2017, thanks to an operation by the Lebanese army. As a result Baalbek has become much safer, has reclaimed its status as a tourist hub and tourism is on the rise again.

However, when I went to Baalbek, the Dutch embassy was advising its citizens not to travel to this mainly Shiite city. On the map on the embassy's website the entire area was marked red to signal great risk. My friend Elie was unconvinced. 'Loads of foreigners go to Baalbek. Just go.'

Thus, an early December morning in 2012, I asked a taxi driver to take me to the 'bus stop for Baalbek'. 'It's that easy', Elie had assured me. When the driver tried to drop me off by the side of the motorway I protested vehemently – there was nothing in sight that looked remotely like a bus stop. The driver, who hardly spoke English but was doing his best to help, pointed to a cluster of white minibuses parked at the side of the motorway. Clearly this emergency lane of the motorway served as a makeshift bus stop for those wanting to go to Baalbek. Moments later, I was continuing my route in one of the minivans. Crammed together against the other passengers – the driver wouldn't leave until all the seats, including the pull-down seats in the centre aisle, were occupied – our vehicle bumped its way eastwards. Breathtaking mountain views and hills covered in vineyards beguiled us. The Beqaa Valley is Lebanon's wine-producing region.

As a foreigner I was a natural target of conversation. There was a typical pattern to every dialogue. First, I was asked where I was from, and my answer always led to an exchange about the current make-up of the Dutch national football team. Because I'm not much of a connoisseur, I was sometimes forced to feign enthusiasm when I couldn't work out which player was being mentioned, if their name was pronounced in an unfamiliar way. Once this topic was exhausted the questions inevitably veered to my age, marital status and number, if any, of children.

Just outside the river town of Zahle, where, according to Elie, you find excellent fish, the minivan driver decided not to go any further towards Baalbek. I assumed that this was because many of the passengers had already disembarked and it made more financial sense for him to transfer the remaining ones to another minivan while he headed back to Beirut.

From the window of the second minivan, which was only half full, I could make out a number of refugee camps. Tents made from rags caught the sunlight. Even from this distance it was possible to see the miserable conditions the Syrians were living in. The snow-topped mountains behind the camps made me imagine how bitterly cold the tents must get at night. The idea haunted me for a long time.

After about half an hour the driver of the second bus, like his predecessor, changed his mind about going to Baalbek. By the time I found a third bus, I started to feel a slight pang of uncertainty as to whether we were still on the main road. Instead of the large, straight dual carriageway that had brought us most of the way since Beirut, we found ourselves on increasingly narrow and dusty paths. The scenery was also different. I noticed posters everywhere of a man whose face I was unfamiliar with back then, as well as a multitude of yellow flags. When I asked the driver for the name of the man on the posters, he brushed my question away as if to tell me to mind my own business. It was obvious that I was in 'Hezbollah country'.

I had done some reading up in preparation for my trip, so I had some notions of the history and politics of Lebanon. In the 1980s, Hezbollah had been involved in kidnappings of foreigners, under the banner of organisations such as the Islamic Jihad. One of their hostages was the Briton, Terry Waite, an envoy of the Archbishop of Canterbury, who was held captive and tortured in a southern suburb of Beirut for five years. What is extraordinary about Waite's story is that he returned to Beirut in 2012, twenty-one years after his release, where he met the prominent Hezbollah leader, Ammar Moussawi (who incidentally denied the involvement of his organisation in the kidnapping), and forgave him. *The Independent* quoted Waite on that day: 'Hezbollah has a negative image in the West and there are those who will accuse me of consorting with terrorists. I would remind such accusers that Hezbollah has grown into a fully-fledged political party with seats in Lebanon's Parliament and is now in a unique position to work for peace in the region.' Was this a case of so-called Stockholm Syndrome, whereby hostages develop an emotional bond with their captors?

I was still thinking about the kidnapping when Baalbek came into view at last. At the foot of the magnificent, awe-inspiring temples I pictured how different the site must have appeared when filled with forty thousand festival-goers. The annual Baalbek Festival attracted top celebrities such as the Lebanese singer Fayrouz, jazz legend Nina Simone and the British pop star Sting, all of whom performed for throngs of fans against the unique backdrop of mountains and Roman temples. Several times, the event had to be relocated to Beirut. During the civil war this was the norm, and after 2012, the festival was moved to the capital again after Baalbek was a target of Syrian rocket attacks. In 2015 the famous festival returned to Baalbek.

Despite the earthquakes in the region, miraculously, the temples are still standing. I had seen ancient temples in Athens and Rome and had visited the ruins in the Egyptian Luxor, but for me, the temple of Bacchus stands out. Not only was I overcome by the sheer size of it, I was also amazed at how intact the remains were. It felt like I was wandering through an actual Roman building. The swarms of tourists that must have roamed here years ago had vanished. Now it was quiet. For several hours, in fact, I was the only visitor. The only human contact I had was with a moustachioed old man who stood guard. He was more than happy to take a couple of pictures with me – it was evidently not the first time he had received such a request. The guard seemed to be quite skilled at taking photographs and chose the perspective that made it look like my head was resting on the ancient columns of the temple of Jupiter in the distance. Only when I was on my way to the exit did I come across four other tourists, who spoke Arabic.

The town of Baalbek itself did not offer much in the way of excitement. A short stroll through the dusty streets took me past little shops selling unremarkable clothes and shoes. It was clearly a poor area. Looking for something to eat in the heart of the town, I came across a simple fast food restaurant that looked clean and modern. I ordered a falafel and took a seat on the first floor, where I complemented the fried chickpea balls with french-fries and coke while 'enjoying' the view of a roundabout. I had not yet discovered the delicious specialties of this region that many local restaurants offer. The 'sfiha Baalbakiya', a freshly-baked pastry stuffed with meat was so alluring that in spite of being a vegetarian, I was persuaded to taste it.

No-one in the restaurant seemed to find the presence of a foreigner unusual. And I, in turn, didn't find the people here much different from those in Beirut, except that almost all of the women in Baalbek were veiled and the men sported conservative-looking beards. Slightly disappointed, I left Baalbek before nightfall. This time the minivan took me straight back to Beirut.

The Shiite movement, Hezbollah has a negative image in the western hemisphere. Not so in Lebanon. Many Shiites support Hezbollah and in areas where Hezbollah has a strong presence, portraits of its leader, Hassan Nasrallah, are ubiquitous. From behind his spectacles he seems to scrutinise the comings and goings. Equally, in these regions, the yellow Hezbollah flag is everywhere. And then, there are the many portraits of the men who died on the battlefield in Syria, often pinned to a tree or lamppost. You will see them on the pictures in the prime of their lives, well groomed, laughing contentedly. Yes, Hezbollah knows how to create propaganda and blast it into Shiite living rooms through its TV station, Al Manar. A few times a year, Nasrallah delivers a speech and Shiite Muslims are glued to their television sets. Whatever he says about the 'Zionists' or the liberation of 'Palestine' always makes news, simply because Hezbollah is stronger than the Lebanese army and Nasrallah, who spends his time between a number of secret shelters, is one of the most powerful men in the land.

Ask Christians in Lebanon what they think of Hezbollah and you will get a range of replies. According to some, the movement is a political partner that helps protect them against Muslim extremists. While Shiite Muslims respect Christians, they say, the same cannot be said for Sunni extremists such as ISIS, who see Christians as heretics who must choose between conversion and the sword. 'But', counters another Christian group, 'if the Iran model is repeated in Lebanon, how much room will be given to other religions?' Jews and Christians are barely tolerated in Iran. Sought-after government jobs are off-limits to them and they are not allowed to celebrate their religious feasts in public places. This fear is one of the reasons why some Christians in Lebanon put their faith in the moderate Sunnis, under the leadership of Saad Hariri, son of the murdered Prime Minister, Rafiq Hariri. While Hariri himself is a moderate, he is propped up by the strict Islamic state of Saudi Arabia, where Sharia law is practiced. Not only is Hariri's party financed by Saudi Arabia, so, at times, is the Lebanese army.

National politics reflect the diverse loyalties of the country's Christians. The Free Patriotic Movement (FPM), of which the President is a member, has a pact with Hezbollah, while the other Christian party, Lebanese Forces, is on the side of Hariri's Sunni followers. Division is the keyword in Lebanese politics. It is therefore not surprising that there exists, besides Hezbollah, a major political movement popular among Shiites, called Amal, meaning 'hope'. This party is older than Hezbollah and counts among its members the influential speaker of the House, Nabih Berri.

Hezbollah is not shy of using the power of marketing. One example of their 'products' is the so-called Hezbollah Museum. A ninety-minute drive from Beirut, the museum is officially called the Mleeta Resistance Tourist Landmark. This centre opened its doors in 2010, exactly ten years after the Israelis pulled out their last troops from Lebanon. One of its main features is to commemorate Hezbollah's victory over the 'Zionists', which came about in 1983 when Israel began its slow withdrawal from Lebanon.

To get to the Hezbollah Museum I deliberately chose a car from Star Taxi who had their office right bellow my lodgings. This taxi company employs only Christian drivers, so it seemed to be a good idea, given the civil relations between most Christians and Hezbollah. My driver was mystified as to why I wanted to visit Mleeta. He kept asking me the reason for my visit. In his twenty-five years of driving taxis, he had never been there.

The mountainous terrain between Saida (Sidon) and Mleeta was unknown territory for my experienced driver. In the last Christian village before entering 'Iran' – as I nicknamed the Shiite territory to the amusement of the driver – he stocked up on water, cigarettes and, at my request, bananas. After this stop he was silent, asking only, to my surprise, if it was really safe for us to go to Mleeta. He frequently needed to asked passers-by for directions, but this is common in Lebanon. Off the main roads, there are very few signposts. Fortunately, the people we approached for directions went out of their way to help us and Mleeta was well-known enough for us to find our route. After about an hour's drive we were finally rewarded with signs for 'Mleeta Tourist Landmark'. The taciturn driver was now showing increasing signs of impatience. Grumbling that it had been a long journey, he wanted to know how long I planned to stay. In response to my offer to join me on my visit of the museum, he said he preferred to nap in the car.

The museum exceeded all my expectations. From the car park you emerge onto a square surrounded by three low-rise buildings painted in a light army-green. Wide steps to the left take you to the top of a hill, while the 'ravine' on the right contains a collection of Israeli weaponry and military vehicles that have been seized by Hezbollah. The ravine is a veritable work of art; it is encircled by a spiral steel construction which leads down into the symbolic abyss.

Fortunately I was assigned an English-speaking guide who, though clean-shaven, was well-versed in the heroic deeds of Hezebollah: how the 'Zionists' had been driven away, after having humiliated the local population by obstructing the supply of food and other essentials to the area. According to my guide, the 'Zionists' were currently repeating their deplorable behaviour in 'Palestine', because that was just their nature. But he was convinced that they would meet the same fate there as they had in Mleeta: utter defeat. He avoided my question about whether the museum had been targeted during the Israeli air raids of 2006. It didn't seem to me to be an irrelevant query, considering that there were still significant tensions on the Lebanese-Israeli border, but when he failed to acknowledge my question a second time, I gave up. Thanking him politely for the tour, I continued viewing the museum on my own.

The museum was full of surprises. The film documentary, which was aired in a state of the art auditorium, featured – and was narrated by – none other than the 'Great Leader', Hassan Nasrallah, himself. I ventured into a tunnel that had been dug to provide shelter from Israeli bombs and followed a path through a forest to the 'enemy', eventually arriving at an observation post. There was also a bunker where visitors could position themselves behind a machine gun. What struck me while viewing the exhibitions was not so much the Israeli weapons on display, but the pictures of Israeli politicians and army officers. These pictures were accompanied by supposed quotations by these men in the Israeli media, in support of the hero's epic of Mleeta: 'I never thought I would live to see this day, when the State and army of Israel, described by its enemies and friends as the undefeatable army, is forced to flee in the face of an Arab party', Yitzhak Shamir, former Prime Minister of Israel, was quoted as saying.

Next to the text was a picture of a coffin draped in the Israeli flag and carried by four Israeli soldiers. The soldiers in the picture were half my age, and fighting in a country that was not theirs. 'What were they doing in Lebanon?' I heard myself think. And that is exactly what the museum pushes you to do: choose a side. 'The good guys against the bad.' Every party claims to be fighting on the side of justice, and there will always be young men who are willing to take up arms for the sake of their ideals or for money. Ninety kilometres to the east of Mleeta, the bloodshed continued between the Syrian army, countless rebel factions and ISIS. And forty-five kilometres to the south there were news reports about knife attacks on Israeli people.

In the souvenir shop I didn't give a second look to the necklaces adorned with real copper bullets. Mleeta means 'where the Earth speaks to heaven'. Could I hear the souls of the dead speaking in this place?' I stood still and looked around. The sky was deep blue, the sun was bright and there was no breeze. Here the Earth almost kissed the heavens. But no, I didn't hear anything. Even the dead didn't beg for peace in this place.

X Jingle Jbeil

Whenever I'm in Lebanon I never fail to pay a visit to Jbeil (Byblos to us foreigners). This coastal town is about a thirty-minute drive from Beirut. Jbeils oldest house dates back to 7000 BC, giving it UNESCO World Heritage status. Rabih had invited Linda and me out to dinner in this magnificent place. And as Rabih has a nose for good restaurants I couldn't wait for this outing. I was also looking forward to it because we were at the end of December and Jbeil, a predominantly Christian city, would be lavishly decorated for Christmas.

Naturally our friend turned up much later than planned to pick us up in Bourj Hammoud. It was around half past eight when we finally drove off so I calculated that we would be sitting down to dinner at about nine. But our young driver decided to take a detour, without consulting any of his friends. Instead of heading directly to Byblos, we first drove up into the hills. He had a surprise planned for us. As I was quite hungry I wasn't particularly enthused by the detour but who was I to turn down a gesture of Lebanese hospitality? More than an hour and a half later we were high up in a mountainous area. Rabih parked the car and we all got out. The freezing air hit us with unexpected force. 'Mar Charbel', Milad whispered. Linda looked questioningly at me. 'Oh, something to do with the Saint Charbel', I said indifferently.

We followed a path further up the hill and there in front of us was the statue of Mar (Saint) Charbel, all in white, on a pedestal, his right arm slightly raised. A woman knelt before the statue to pray. Other visitors stood still for a few moments and then walked on. Nobody spoke.

Nearby was the Mar Maroun monastery, where the hermit, Charbel Makhlouf (1828-1898), drew his final breath. He is believed to have performed many miracles in his lifetime, including healing the sick. The monastery was painted a beautiful bright yellow. No monks lived there anymore; since Saint Charbel's death the monastery has been functioning as a monument to honour him. On one of the walls, the Star of Bethlehem shows the way. Rabih, whose father is a Muslim, whose mother is a Christian and whose grandmother a Polish Jew, whispered that he had been visiting the monastery regularly, to pray and to immerse himself in its peace.

I sauntered through the passages of the monastery, falling increasingly under its charm. Mar Charbel had the feel of a holy place with a great sense of the mystical. Later I realised that this sensation must have come from the fact that the other visitors regarded the monastery as sacred and behaved accordingly. Rabih whispered to us that he was going to pray for a sick person. He found a place at the front of the chapel. I stood behind him and followed his example. I was surprised at how easy and natural it was for me to pray for someone in need. For me, Mar Charbel is the most mystical and thus most beautiful place in Lebanon.

It was not until we were back in the car that we started talking again. The visit had entranced all four of us and Linda fully agreed with me that this place had something magical about it. Were there spirits wondering around in Mar Charbel? It was nearly half past ten when at last we sat down for dinner in the overcrowded restaurant. Foenicia, as expected, turned out to be an excellent choice of Rabih's. After dinner we took a night-time stroll through the winter wonderland. Although there was no snow, Jbeil was transformed, as every year at Christmastime, into a fairytale land. In the picturesque heart of this city, all the houses around the old Roman excavations were illuminated. In the centre stood a thirty-metre high golden Christmas tree, which could also be admired from inside. Instead of branches, this festive creation had gold-painted leaves attached to it. At the very top was a large white cross that was visible from a distance. It is not surprising that in 2014 this tree made the second place in the Wall Street Journal's photos of special Christmas trees around the world. Every evening during the Christmas period, thousands of people came to see the tree. Linda and I felt like we had landed in a Christmas fairy tale. This was the Lebanon I loved so much.

XI Walking tours with Ronnie

Ronnie Chatah was a phenomenon in Beirut. Every Sunday he led a group of tourists to discover the city. The visitors would assemble near the Emirates head office, pay twenty dollars for the tour and traipse after Ronnie into the little side streets. I joined Ronnie's tour twice. The first time, it was a delightful and enlightening experience because Lebanon was still new to me. When I walked with him a year later, in August 2013, Lebanon had become considerably less safe. For Ronnie too, life changed dramatically that year.

The first time I visited Lebanon, the country was relatively stable. The massive influx of Syrian refugees had not yet begun, there were no terrorist attacks and the number of tourists visiting the country was actually on the rise. For the first stop of his tour, Ronnie invited his thirty-odd visitors to take a seat on the wide steps in front of the Lebanese central bank, *Banque du Liban*. 'I'm going to start out by showing you my passport', he began in his distinct American accent, 'or you won't believe me'. The young, blond, blue-eyed and pale-skinned man in his twenties then held up a Lebanese passport.

Full of outrageous stories, Ronnie was extremely entertaining and made his version of the city tour unique by taking his groups to the narrow hidden alleys and lesser known places of interest.

On the other side of an unremarkable alley, you might suddenly be treated to a colossal, beautifully preserved Ottoman-French style building dating back to the beginning of the nineteenth century. Moments later you might find yourself in front of a completely dilapidated house belonging to a family that fled abroad during the Civil War. Ronnie knew a lot about Lebanon and was keen to share his knowledge. I learned from him that this tiny Mediterranean country has no less than eighteen religions, that the Lebanese President is always a Christian and that one can always pay in US dollars without the risk of being cheated, because the exchange rate is firmly fixed at fifteen hundred Lebanese pounds to the dollar. His five-hour tour serves as a kind of crash course on Lebanon.

One of the highlights was the former Holiday Inn hotel, of which only the concrete skeleton remained. The excitement was building before we even approached it. Ronnie warned us that we could take photos of the ruin from where we stood, but no closer. As we draw nearer the soldiers on guard would notice us and prohibit any more photos. The Holiday Inn, after all, was a military facility these days and for Lebanese soldiers, any camera was treated like an enemy.

The second time I joined Ronnie on a tour, there were only twelve participants. Our guide observed that it was the smallest group he had had in years. Among the tourists was my travelling companion, Stijn, who was visiting Lebanon for the first time. Ronnie's cautious optimism from a year earlier had now completely vanished. The security situation was deteriorating day by day. A week earlier, bombs had exploded in south Beirut which is home to many Shiites. Dozens of people had died. 'Many people have decided not to come today and I can't rule out the possibility that this tour will be my last.' Ronnie's voice was sombre. 'I don't know if I can guarantee your safety next week.' In a strange way, the sight of the gutted hotel had a reassuring effect on me. 'It won't ever get that bad here again, will it?' asked Stijn, who had travelled through Somalia as a journalist with heavily-armed militias and was no stranger to violence. I didn't reply, but listened for the second time to the extraordinary story of this iconic building. At its inauguration in 1973 the Holiday Inn was one of the most luxurious hotels in the region. But its function as a hotel was short lived because the outbreak of the Civil War in 1975 bestowed on the building – being the tallest near the centre of Beirut – strategic importance. Whoever had possession of the building could take aim at their opponents, who were all fighting to seize the city centre, from the top floors. Virtually all the warring factions had occupied the hotel at one stage or another. Yasser Arafat with his PLO men was one example, as was the Syrian army. Whoever held the building had the winning hand in the Civil War. Although the War is over, possession of the building still has symbolic importance. As soon as the last wartime occupier moved out, the Lebanese army units moved in.

Somehow we were authorised to enter the area behind the former Ottoman palace, which houses the office of the Lebanese Prime Minister, without much trouble. Clearly Ronnie had some very highly-placed connections. A short chat with the uniformed guards, who consulted their superiors by phone, was sufficient. 'We are now in what used to be the Jewish quarter', Ronnie announced as we wandered through Wadi Abou Jamiel, which, before the reconstruction of Beirut, was known as Hag al-Yahoud (Yahoud means Jewish). We were then regaled with an account of an extraordinary woman who lived in this neighbourhood, which before the Civil War (1975-1990) was the heart of Jewish Lebanon. Her name was Lisa Srour, and she lived in a completely rundown apartment together with her many cats. Whenever she caught sight of Ronnie with a group of tourists, she would shout out to them: 'I am the last Jew in Lebanon!' and proceeded to amuse the tourists with outrageous anecdotes. Lisa had allegedly met all the great policy-makers in the world and had indirectly initiated peace negotiations between Israel and Palestine. But we would not have the chance to be entertained by this astonishing character, as Lisa had tragically passed away a few years before. 'She said she was the last Jew in Lebanon. Are there really then no Jews left?', Stijn wanted to know. According to Ronnie, there probably still were some, but not more than a few dozen. Jewish people in Lebanon are careful not to flaunt their ethnicity so the exact figures are not known, he explained, and left the conversation at that.

I had learnt from Ronnie's LinkedIn profile that the topic of his university thesis was the Jewish diaspora in Syria and Iraq. So, when we were at the end of our long tour, I asked him bluntly if I could read his thesis. We were standing next to the statue of the journalist Samir Kassir, who had advocated for a truly inde-pendent Lebanon without interference from neighbouring Syria and who had been assassinated in 2005. Ronnie, who until that moment, had been so open and talkative, turned deathly pale on hearing my question. He now seemed hardly able to speak at all. Eventually, he stammered that the thesis was not available to the public and that he didn't want to discuss it. 'In fact', he continued, 'this whole conversation did not happen.' I was quite taken aback by his reaction. The conversation did not happen? Stijn too was bewildered but neither of us could figure out why there had been such a change in the young man's demeanour. Once home, I tried to make contact with Ronnie through LinkedIn, but he never responded to my invitation.

Later that year, on another visit to Lebanon, I was watching a live funeral service on TV. A smartly-dressed young man was addressing the mourners. Looking closely, I recognised the man in the suit: it was Ronnie! Why would my young guide be addressing a funeral, live on TV? Then it dawned on me. Ronnie was speaking at the funeral of his father. He was the son of Mohammed Chatah, former ambassador to the United States (which explained Ronnie's American accent), former vice chairman of the Central Bank and an influential voice in Lebanese politics. Chatah was associated with the Sunni Future Movement. According to Elie, Chatah was one of the few Sunni political figures in Lebanon who had a good relationship with Hezbollah. An economist, he advocated for a liberal democracy which would give room to all religions in Lebanon. His dreams came to a brutal end on 27 December 2013, at about nine-forty in the morning, when a fifty-kilo car bomb hidden in a stolen Honda exploded in downtown Beirut. Besides the politician, eight bystanders also lost their lives, and seven more were injured.

When Elie came home from work that day I told him about the funeral and about Ronnie. I explained how I knew him and suspected, because of his first name and his interest in the pre-war Jewish community in Lebanon, that he belonged to the 'Israelites', the name of the Jewish sect in Lebanon. Immediately, a conspiracy theory was born – a typical Middle-eastern habit! Elie claimed that Chatah was indeed a Jewish surname and he remembered having seen it on voters' lists where the voter's religion was displayed. I found out that he was not wrong: the name Chattah (with a double 't') appears on the list of Jewish-Lebanese names which was drawn up in the publication *Les Juifs du Liban* by the writer Fred Anzarouth (which can be found online). When transcribed from Arabic into the Latin script, Chatah is sometimes spelled with a single 't'.

However, there were still some questions that puzzled me. Why would a Jewish man be named Mohammed? Elie's explanation was that the family may have officially converted to Islam for safety reasons, but without turning their backs on Judaism in practice – he also knew a 'Druze' who was actually Jewish. In support of his theory is the name of Chatah's wife: Nina. Not an Islamic name at all. On the other hand, his other son was called Omar, which is definitely not Jewish. Elie reported that the Chatahs were under the protection of the powerful (Sunni) Hariri family. In my opinion there was a link between the Chatah family and Judaism, but I am hesitant to fully embrace Elie's drastic conclusions.

After his father's assassination, Ronnie stopped doing the tours. The fear he had expressed in my presence – that the deteriorating situation in Lebanon would eventually make it impossible for such tourist activities to continue – had cruelly become reality, and for him in a very personal way. But just as Beirut rose from its ashes following the Civil War, Ronnie too has re-entered the stage. I saw on his website that he has resumed the tours since 2018. I would highly recommend anyone visiting Beirut to join one of them. Just don't ask him anything about his thesis.

XII Tariq from Sour

Sometime during my second trip to Lebanon, one of the two rental rooms at my regular address became available. Elie and Tofik would have no problem finding a lodger. Selecting the perfect, exemplary tenant, however, was more of a challenge. In comparison, selecting players for the Dutch national football team was a piece of cake. Elie would not even consider any Syrian applicants. 'Too many problems', apparently, although he wouldn't elaborate on the nature of those problems. There was a clear preference for a tenant from Europe. For one thing, it enabled him to practise his English or French and to expand his knowledge of the world outside of the Middle East. Another strong reason, no doubt, was that Europeans were financially much better off than most Syrians. This resulted in a well-stocked fridge, from which Elie had no qualms about helping himself. When the chocolate and yoghurt I bought kept mysteriously vanishing, I soon decided to hide my supplies elsewhere!

I had no idea what sort of people booked accommodation through Airbnb and Facebook. Elie did ask my advice about a fifty-year old Belgian applicant who was in Beirut to do voluntary work with children. Without really thinking, I said, 'Oh, be careful. You don't want to have a paedophile in the house.' I admit that that conclusion was premature but Elie had already crossed out his name. The two candidates who passed the first stage of the selection were a young Norwegian man who had come to study in Lebanon and, interestingly enough, a twenty-three year old Lebanese man called Tariq. Neither Elie nor Tofik was enthusiastic about Lebanese tenants, as apparently they were unreliable when it came to paying their rent. Perhaps Tariq's remarkably good looks (lush black hair, strong masculine features, gentle gaze) had swayed them this time?

At any rate, Tariq was scheduled to come over that evening to meet them. As Tofik was busy cleaning the kitchen and Elie was in the shower, it was my privilege to welcome the visitor. Over the intercom he had sounded confused, which didn't surprise me as he would have had to find his way through the maze of nameless streets to get to Elie's house. Tariq told me he had parked his car in front of the Inaye church, following Elie's instructions. That's how it works in Lebanon – nobody uses street names, it's easier to meet at landmarks like churches, schools or mosques. Not a bad idea in theory, but it doesn't always work. Once, having arranged to meet a friend outside a church, I stood waiting opposite *Saint Michel* while he was waiting for me near *Saint Michael*. The two almost identically named churches were within fifty metres of each other. When I look back at it now, it is quite hilarious but at the time I was rather annoyed.

In any case, meeting up with friends in Lebanon is a challenge. While Dutch people would normally meet in the front of a particular landmark, Lebanese people tend to wait just around the corner. Thus, when I walked towards the Inaye Church I didn't spot Tariq immediately, but diagonally opposite I noticed a four-wheel-drive (double-parked, of course!) with its full headlights on. 'Martin?' asked the driver. I was instantly under his spell. 'What a charming young man!' For some reason, I thought he looked more Iranian than Lebanese, which is absurd because I don't know any Iranians and have never even been to Iran. Perhaps it has something to do with his skin and hair which were darker than that of most Lebanese people. I shook his hand and escorted him to the apartment.

The meeting with Elie and Tofik was very brief as Tariq was driving down that afternoon to visit his family in Sour in southern Lebanon (also known by its Roman name, Tyrus). Within ten minutes of his being in the apartment, Tariq and I had swapped telephone numbers. This is common practice in Lebanon. Even after a short exchange with someone in the street you might leave with their number. As I was showing him out again, I mentioned that I was keen to visit Sour. "If I'm there at the same time as you I will be happy to show you around', he smiled. After he had gone I felt perturbed. I was anxious to see Tariq again but the chance seemed remote as Elie had his mind set on letting the room out to the tall Norwegian. That same Tuesday evening I sent Tariq a message saying that I planned to visit Sour the following Thursday. Would he be around then? The reply came almost immediately: 'Ahla wa sahla'. Welcome.

Two days later, in the early morning, I began my journey towards the south of the country. The city of Sour is situated near the border with Israel in an area controlled by Hezbollah. In the old days, there were trains between Beirut and Sour, and even further – to Haifa and Tel Aviv. Then the hostility between the two countries led to the destruction of the railways by bombs and grenades during the Civil War. So the first step of my trip was a taxi from Bourj Hammoud to the Cola 'bus station' in the south of Beirut. Not exactly a bus station, Cola is more like a gathering point where minivans arrive and depart, where temporary eateries spring up and then disappear again and where Syrian refugees flog water and sesame bagel-type breads to travellers. There are no signboards providing passengers with information about destinations or departures times. It is up to each one to find their way.

Having asked several people for a direct bus to Sour, I was about to give up when a man with a thick beard gesticulated wildly for me to hurry into a minivan. 'Yalla, yalla!' he shouted, as if time were running out. I rushed into the van, only to find that it was only partly full. As it was a warm winter, I decided to step out again and wait outside, to the disapproval of the bearded man who urged me to get back in. It seemed to be his job to fill the van as quickly as possible. I gave him a friendly smile but ignored his entreaties. When the bus was almost full I got back on and a little while later we were on our way to the city of Sour, which was founded by the Phoenicians in 2750 BC.

But of course this was not a direct bus to Sour. Instead of the motorway, the driver chose the bumpy coastal road. The route took us past hotels, banana plantations and little villages that were not mentioned in my guidebook. The view was magnificent throughout the drive which kept us in constant sight of the sea. We arrived in Sour with only a thirty minute delay (Elie had told me the trip takes about an hour).

In contrast to the one in Cola, the bus station in Sour looked much more like one you might expect to see in Europe. It was extremely well-organised and featured an official entrance and exit and even information boards. Tariq was nowhere to be seen. I had sent him a text message to say that I was delayed – could he really be even later than I was? This was Lebanon after all. Perhaps he was still looking for a free parking spot in order to meet me at the bus station. But I was still thinking along Dutch lines. In fact Tariq had waited until he had received my arrival text before leaving his house in a village just outside Sour, so I found myself waiting another thirty minutes. If this had happened in Holland I would have been irritated, but not here. I stood in the warm winter sun, quivering with the anticipation of exploring this new city, which glistened invitingly, like a pearl waiting for me to discover it, and I was not in a mood to be annoyed.

Seeing Tariq again was thrilling. We kissed each other on the cheek as is the custom for men in Lebanon. It felt as if I had known him for years. Immediately I got the same feeling I had had the last time I had been in his presence. What a beautiful man he was! Despite the relaxed atmosphere, there was slight tension in the air. As soon as we had stepped into his four-wheel drive, Tariq started telling me about himself and about his region. His family had been there for generations. He is one of the few Sunnis in an area mostly inhabited by Shiites. There were also some Christians, he explained, who sold alcohol on the beach in the summer for anyone who wanted to buy it. The beaches in Sour are impeccably clean, Tariq pointed out, unlike those in most of Lebanon. He was proud of his city, and with good reason.

Tariq took me directly from the bus station to what could be described as the Rome of Lebanon. There were Roman tombs, pillars, a well-preserved triumphal arc and a vast hippodrome of which a part of the gallery was still intact. I was overwhelmed by these vestiges and simultaneously struck by the how much of a common history this city had with Europe. What is more, Greek legend says that the goddess, Europa, was born in Sour. My companion seemed to be an expert on classical antiquity. His knowledge surpassed mine, in spite of my advanced classical education and history degree. Tariq admired Alexander the Great, who in the fourth century AD made a decision that has had a determining effect on Sour to the present day. The great warrior connected the island just off the coast, a thriving Phoenician city, with the coastal trading town of Ushu. Tariq told me all this, as we ambled along the extensive Roman cobblestoned road, which would have been under water until Alexander the Great's arrival. I could not imagine how it was possible for them to reclaim land from the Mediterranean Sea without modern equipment. Tariq, for once, didn't have an answer to this either.

As we walked, I kept wondering if Tariq was gay. I knew he was keen to share a house with with Elie and Tofik, who were openly gay, but did this mean that he shared their sexual orientation? It was certainly possible, but somehow he didn't come across that way at all. Strangely, this made him even more attractive to me. As we stood under the deserted gallery of the Roman hippodrome, for a split second I imagined what it would be like to take his hand or even kiss him. But I dismissed the thought immediately. Right from the start, Tariq had made it clear that he was well-known in Sour and his spending an afternoon with a foreigner would not go unnoticed. If anyone asked, he said, he would tell them that he knew me from the university, where I had (according to his story), worked for a while. In other words, he wanted me to be discreet. I got the message.

Following our long stroll among the ancient ruins, Tariq had another surprise in store. He took me to the Christian quarter right along the coast where the facades of the houses are painted in striking colours. We shared a drink in a grand café on the nearby harbour watching the slow sunset. It was almost romantic. On the next table sat a number of French soldiers from Unifil, the UN peacekeeping mission that has been in place in Lebanon since

1978. It is their task to prevent hostilities between Lebanon and Israel. In 1979, the Netherlands made its contribution by sending troops as part of that mission. They stayed there for six years, often in harsh conditions because of the many outbursts of violence during the then raging Civil War.

Some of the French soldiers stood out because of their dark skin, which is a rarity in Lebanon.

It suddenly occurred to me that this location would be an ideal target for a terrorist attack, causing many fatalities among the French soldiers. But as I looked over at Tariq and saw the sun disappearing behind the harbour, I decided that this was a beautiful day.

On my return trip, which went much faster than the outward journey since we took the motorway, my mind was still on Tariq. Would I ever see him again? What if Elie and Tofik decided not to take him on as their tenant? As we drew into southern Beirut at slow speed due to a traffic jam, we passed a building with heavily-armed bearded men standing outside. Automatic weapons hung over their chests. Elie later told me that it must have been a building owned by Hezbollah, as that was the only group in Lebanon, besides the army, that allows its men to carry weapons. Less than a week later, on 2 January 2014, a car bomb ripped through the Shiite neighbourhood of Harat Hreik, which I had passed through on my way back from Sour. Its target was the Hezbollah headquarters. Four people were killed and seventy-seven wounded. Although it was a different Hezbollah building to the one I had seen on my way back from Sour, I still had the sensation that I had narrowly escaped death.

There was more bad news, albeit of a totally different nature. As I had feared, Elie was set on letting out the room to the Norwegian man. Having a Lebanese person as a tenant would be asking for problems, he claimed. And to make things worse, Tariq was from the south. Could he really be trusted? Had he meant it when he said he didn't mind living in a house that was owned by a gay couple? And what about his friends, would they be tolerant towards gays when they came to visit him? Tofik favoured having Tariq as a tenant and an argument between the two men ensued. In the end they left the decision up to me, and that is how it came about that Tariq moved in with Elie and Tofik, and became a friend for life.

XIII The Hidden Synagogue

Since my very first visit to Lebanon I have been hearing stories about the hidden synagogue. Every Saturday, somewhere in the mountains, in the heart of Druze country, Jews allegedly come together to celebrate the Sabbath. If this story is true it would make this *shul* the last Jewish temple still in use in Lebanon. Elie told me about it when I first visited Lebanon but he didn't know its exact location. So one day we decided to search for the hidden synagogue.

Elie was tipped-off by his friend, Omar, whom I had met several times. Omar is from a well-off Druze family who apparently lived in a village close to the synagogue. It was said that many people knew of its existence but they all kept silent about it.

The Druze and the Jews have a complex relationship. Although the Lebanese Druze leader, Walid Jumblatt, does not in any way show support for Israel, the people of his tribe living in Israel, the Israeli Druze, are loyal to their State and even serve in the Israeli army. The question is whether Jumblatt and other Druze leaders are in contact with their people on the other side of the border. This would actually be forbidden in Lebanon. Some Druze men have been known to have travelled to Israel, for example to marry a Druze woman.

It was on a Sabbath day in 2015 – which also happened to be Pesach (the Jewish Easter) – that Milad drove us on our quest. Milad is a very tall and skinny young Protestant man. Elie, who was drawn to Judaism (but not to Israel), had brought along three yarmulkes in case we succeeded in finding the synagogue and were allowed to enter. These Jewish skullcaps could not be purchased in Lebanon and had been given to Elie by friends from abroad. I wondered how we would explain why we had them in our possession if we were stopped and searched at a checkpoint. Elie insisted that, as Judaism was one of the eighteen official religions in Lebanon, the yarmulkes were not forbidden. I prayed he was right but was equally convinced that the Lebanese police were more likely to regard us as spies for Israel. Although we had often been stopped at checkpoints during previous trips, we were lucky that the car had never been searched. The probability of it happening now seemed very slim indeed, in fact just as slim as the chance of us finding our synagogue.

And so we started out off Beirut in Milad's old dented car, first towards the south along the coast and twenty minutes later we turned into the mountains towards Beiteddine. An hour's drive from Beirut, Beiteddine is the location of the presidential summer residence and a museum which is well worth a visit. As we entered a built-up area, Elie suddenly shouted 'Stop, here it is!' Milad stopped the car abruptly. We got out and looked around but I didn't see any synagogue. Elie had spotted a Star of David on the front of a house. Upon closer inspection we found Elie's discovery to be an eight-pointed star, the symbol of the Druze. Naturally, Elie didn't have an address. Omar had merely told him that the synagogue – if it even existed – was somewhere in this area. I looked at Milad, whose expression reflected what I was thinking: this was a wild goose chase. But Elie had already identified another building that, according to him, was almost certainly used as a synagogue. The building towered high above the town and we had to climb a long flight of steps to reach it. When at last we were standing in front of the huge structure, it was something of an anticlimax. There didn't seem to be anything distinctive about it. We couldn't look inside as all the windows were firmly shuttered, but this is not unusual in the Middle East. As we stood, closely examining every detail of the building, I began to get nervous about arousing suspicion. And with good reason. A woman further up the street suddenly called out to us in English. 'Yalla, yalla, quick, quick come to see the synagogue!' We couldn't believe our ears and hurried towards her and the old building where she was standing. A nimble woman of roughly sixty years old, she was willing to let us have a look inside the temple. She said that we were in luck; as a rule, tourists were not permitted inside. The exterior looked like that of any other Lebanese building; a kind of two-storey shoebox with two doors of solid wood and four windows. When Elie produced the yarmulkes, the woman showed delight and surprise. 'Yahoudi?' She wanted to know if we were Jewish. Elie replied something in Arabic that I couldn't make out. It was then that I saw two men working in the building at the other side of the entrance. Elie greeted them: 'Shabbat shalom!' to which they replied with the same words. They were both wearing beards according to the Jewish orthodox tradition with a shawl around their shoulders that reminded me of the *tallit*, a Jewish prayer shawl. Meanwhile, our hostess warned us that we would only be allowed in for a short time as the synagogue was about to close for the remainder of the day. Absolutely nothing in the building was evocative of a synagogue. The arches made it look more like a wine cellar. However, I did notice a cut-away in the wall, which might have housed the ark to store the Torah rolls. Unsurprisingly we were hurriedly ushered out even before we had the chance to address the workmen.

Immediately after, the woman led us to a place near where she lived. It was a chapel with statues of Mary all around. Under the watchful eye of the Blessed Virgin, our guide displayed her wares: homemade drinks, such as rose water, which is used in all kinds of recipes, and soap. There was also a sofa and a television set. Clearly, she used the chapel as her living room. We, however, were more interested in the synagogue and the Jewish community of the town but she kept bringing our attention back to the products she was selling. All we were able to find out from her was what we already suspected, that the synagogue had been sold a very long time ago. It was now being managed by the French cultural institute, Alliance Française, which, together with the local authorities, was attempting to restore it to its original state.

Then it was back to the exceptional quality of her rose water, and the fact her products were used in restaurants all over Beirut. I made another attempt to steer the conversation back and asked her how many Jews still lived in the town. 'None', was her reply. 'They all moved to Israel.' And the sales pitch began again. I finally asked her whether the new building that we thought to be a synagogue was used as a Jewish house of worship. It was not, she said. A doctor's family was living there now. And yet again, she changed the subject back to her wares. I gave up. The woman had kindly helped us to find the old synagogue, and I felt obliged to buy something from her. I chose two bottles of rose water and a few bars of soap and we left the chapel.

Despite Milad's and my objections, Elie wanted to go back to the house he had originally thought to be the hidden synagogue. We walked around the building again and then Elie noticed something intriguing. In one of the walls of the house was what looked like an air vent, but if you looked from a certain angle the Star of David became distinguishable. There was no doubt: this had to be the hidden synagogue. While we walked back to the car, feeling euphoric, I noticed a hairdressing salon called David and later a clothing shop by the name of Suleiman (the Arabic equivalent of the Jewish Solemon). Could it be possible that this town still had a considerable number of Jewish inhabitants? Or was I imagining things?

Elie tried, but Omar didn't have anything to say about the hidden synagogue. Not even to confirm whether we had found it or not. Elie later revealed that Omar's mother was Jewish, and thus Halaka (the body of Jewish religious laws) stipulated that he too belonged to the faith. Doubts sprung up in me again. Was the woman in the chapel really a Christian? Or had she found, under the protection of the Virgin, the perfect hiding place for a Jew?

XIV On the run

While I was staying at Elie's, many refugees passed through his house. Most of them were newcomers and had just arrived from Syria. They had found my friend through word of mouth in the gay community and Elie was always happy to offer them a place on his couch for a few nights.

I remember a young man named Sebastian, a committed atheist who was determined to settle in the Czech Republic, as he had learned that was the country with the highest percentage of atheists. Another was a Syrian, Jean, from the district of Latakia, who had been selected by UNHCR to be taken to a safe country. There was also John, an outspoken Syrian who after his arrival in Lebanon had converted to Christianity and had posted pictures of Jesus all over his Facebook page. John never stayed over; he just dropped in now and then, especially when he needed something. It was quite a colourful crowd. What these men had in common is that they all wanted to travel to Europe. This was before the summer of 2015: before the walls had been built in Eastern Europe. Syrians could still take the boat from Tripoli to Turkey and the latter hadn't yet promised the EU it would prevent refugees from making the crossing over into Greece.

Twenty-eight year-old Samir was tall and skinny with pale skin and jet-black hair. When I met him in December 2015 he had only been in Lebanon for a week. Through the Airbnb website, he had found himself at Elie and Tofik's house. In spite of their reservations regarding Syrians as tenants, Samir had made it through the selection process. One evening, while I was washing the dishes and he was making an omelette in the kitchen, he told me his story. He didn't have a choice but to flee. He had worked in a hotel in Damascus and had learned English by speaking to foreign guests. But because of the war, the number of hotel guests had greatly diminished. His earnings had plunged and he lived in fear of being drafted to serve in Assad's army. Going back to his village in north Syria was not an option as the economy was in tatters. Being a soldier was the only way to earn a liveable wage, unless you joined ISIS, and Samir knew men who had done this, purely in order to sustain their families. If another terrorist group offered more money, their allegiance would switch instantly. 'Only foreign combatants sign on with ISIS because of their belief in the Islamic caliphate', Samir stated drily, as he slid his omelette onto a piece of flat Lebanese bread. He took his plate to his room to eat alone. I had never seen him eat anything other than bread, eggs and tinned vegetables. He was also a chain smoker, but who could blame him? Cigarettes are extremely affordable in Lebanon.

The next morning I was in the living room, balancing my laptop on my knees, when I saw Samir going out. Dressed in a drab pair jeans and a striped shirt he was on his way to find a job in a hotel. In the afternoon he was back, disillusioned and defeated. 'They all need to hire workers but nobody wants an illegal immigrant', he said glumly. None of the hotel owners would risk the fine they could get for employing him. Moreover, if he happened to get caught in a police raid he would most likely be imprisoned. While in Europe you cannot extradite refugees to war-torn countries, there was no such protection for them in Lebanon. A change of policy came only after considerable pressure from the international community.

Samir's only course then, was to obtain a work permit and for that he would have to sell his only possession: his laptop. Bribing a public servant was his only recourse and it wasn't cheap. Once he had a job he could start saving for the crossing to Turkey. There were daily ferry crossings from the port of Tripoli in north Lebanon but Samir was out of luck again as Turkey had just done away with the law that enabled Syrians to travel to that country without a visa. In addition, rumours were brewing about the Hungarian Prime Minister, Orban, building a wall on the border with Serbia and Croatia to stop refugees from entering Hungary.

The next day Samir had a visit from his friend Mohammed, who was a few years younger than him and studied engineering. Mohammed came bearing a box of sweet delicacies from Syria, which Samir insisted were much tastier than the Lebanese equivalents. As he gratefully savoured one in his mouth, I remembered having recently read that there was a serious shortage of sugar in Syria, leading to the price of this commodity soaring, and it seemed even more decadent for us to enjoy these delicious sweet luxuries.

Mohammed was clearly from a wealthy family. He was well-dressed and had initially booked himself into a hotel for his short stay in Beirut, but Samir persuaded his friend to stay with him in order to save money. Mohammed had planned to finish his studies in Germany and had travelled with valid documents from Damascus to Beirut. He had an appointment at the German embassy the next day. Being a student, he was exempt from military service, so he didn't have to worry about being forced to serve in the Syrian army. Mohammed had a carefree air about him and I wondered if that was just a facade. In two days time he would take the bus back to Damascus. As it was his friend's first time in Beirut, Samir wanted to show him the city's highlights and in the evening they went out clubbing. I heard them returning home at four o'clock the next morning. Two young friends coming home from a night out, a little drunk and chatting about girls: it appeared so normal. The war seemed further away than ever.

After Mohammed – who, unlike Samir, was not much of a talker – returned to Damascus, I had a very interesting conversation with my fellow tenant from Syria. To my question about which country he eventually wanted to settle in he answered that the UK sprang to mind as he already spoke English and he had a cousin living there. Germany also appealed to him as he had heard that refugees there are given money and accommodation. 'What about somewhere like Portugal?' I offered. He looked puzzled at my suggestion. I explained that countries with relatively few refugees might have a more lenient asylum procedure. Furthermore, he looked a bit Portuguese and wouldn't stand out there. Finally, the climate in Portugal was not very different from that in Syria. His dark green eyes sparkled at the prospect. I might have given him an idea. A while later I was searching the internet on this subject. I accidentally found out that Brazil had an open door policy for Syrians and ran a special programme for them. But Samir was worried that learning Portuguese would be too much of an obstacle and doubted whether there would be other Syrians in those countries who could help him.

Sebastian eventually took a rubber dingy from Turkey to Greece and reached his dream destination, the Czech Republic. On Facebook the twenty year-old looks happy in his new country.

All I know of Jean is that he lives in Norway now, but I am not in contact with him.

John successfully acquired a permit to live in Denmark, via a UNHCR scheme for the most vulnerable refugees (like Jean, John is gay), and lived in Aarhus. But, as he told me, the Danish culture clashed with his own, and he subsequently asked for asylum in the Netherlands in 2017 under a new identity. This is remarkable because the fingerprints database used by European countries would normally make this impossible. He currently works in a hotel in the Netherlands and is fairly happy.

Samir still lives in Beirut. His first job as a waiter, sometimes working for fifteen hours a day, barely kept him going and it was only thanks to tips from customers that he was able to get by. A few years ago he began teaching Arabic to foreigners and found that this endeavour paid well. He has moved to a nice apartment in a middle class, Christian neighbourhood of Beirut, that he shares with foreign students and expats. At the moment of writing, March 2018, he still hasn't been awarded a residence permit.

XV Trouble in Trablous

'*Where* did you go?! What?! Unbelievable! I wouldn't go there in a thousand years!'

These were some of the reactions of my friends when I told them that I had been on a day trip to the country's second biggest city, Tripoli. Most people from Beirut don't find the idea of visiting Trablous – as the city is called in Arabic – alluring. If you have to go there, it is usually for business or family obligations. Only an hour's drive north of the capital (in the rare event that there are no traffic jams), Trablous should be attractive to visitors. The day can start with a peaceful ramble through the picturesque old souq followed by a stopover at the citadel which overlooks the city. Just as Jerusalem in Israel is the photo negative of Tel Aviv, Trablous contrasts with Beirut. It is devotion (*memento mori*), in the former, versus hedonism (seize the day), in the latter. In the traditional and conservative Trablous, there are no casinos, no glamorous night-clubs and in most areas, no alcohol. Few tourists visit the city, but this is not due to its conservative character.

There have been sectarian tensions between residents of the districts of Jabal Mohsen and Bab al-Tabaneh. Hostility between these two factions, which were already diametrically opposed to one another since the Lebanese civil war, had intensified with the war in Syria. Alawis, who live on the Jabal Mohsen hill, support the Syrian President Assad. They belong to one of the eighteen official religions in Lebanon, which entitles them to be represented in the Parliament. Syria has a far more extensive Alawi community. For centuries, the Alawi have been persecuted by Sunni Muslims, whose extremists regard them as heretics. The Alawi religion is put in the same category as Shiite Islam as both religions regard Ali, the son-in-law of Mohammed, as the first imam.

In Trablous, the Alawi district is next to the Sunni Bab al-Tabbaneh district. The two areas are divided by a street which is appropriately named 'Syria'. In 2014, a security plan was implemented and the Sunni and Alawi leaders agreed to end the skirmishes. Ever since there has been – with the exception of some minor incidents – peace between the two groups.

It was in the summer of 2014 that I had decided to visit the city. It was relatively peaceful in that period and I wanted to seize the opportunity. To me it seemed odd to have seen almost the whole of Lebanon with the exception of its second city. My friend Elie was the only Lebanese friend willing to accompany me. Petter, an extremely tall, blond Swede, who was staying temporarily at Elie's, was keen to join us. I wasn't particularly happy about that, knowing that Petter's stature and pale features would attract unnecessary attention, but I didn't have a good enough reason to object. The previous day, when I had taken it upon myself to show Petter around the neighbourhood, I had been surprised by the constant calls of 'Hello Sir! Where are you from?' that followed us. This had never happened to me before, and it made me realise how little I myself stood out in Beirut. Not particularly tall, I don't look very much like a typical northern European, particularly when I hide my blue eyes behind a pair of sunglasses. So when, at the last minute, digestive problems made Petter decide not to join us on our trip to Trablous, I have to admit I was relieved.

We took the bus in the hot, late afternoon and arrived in Lebanon's second city around four o'clock. The sunlight bounced off the typical Ottoman-style buildings in the main square, but in three hours it would be dark. When I got off the bus I saw some older men squatting in the street, drinking thimble-sized cups of coffee. This was not an uncommon sight in the Middle East, but it was Ramadan! Was Tripoli then less strict than I had been led to believe?

Elie had arranged for a tour guide, a Palestinian named Mohammed, whom he had met once before in Beirut. Mohammed was a twenty year-old student and, as I found out shortly afterwards, was bisexual and a devout Muslim. The thoughtful young man encouraged us to find something to drink, but out of solidarity we decided to postpone that until after sunset. Mohammed was full of energy. After wandering through the narrow and quiet (because of Ramadan) streets of the charming old souq, we neared the hammam (bathhouse), where a group of youngsters ostentatiously offered to give us a massage in that establishment. We declined politely.

During our walk I felt my vocational impulse come to the fore. I asked our guide to show us the place where, on 23 August 2013, two bombs had exploded simultaneously at the exact moment that worshippers were leaving the house of prayer, causing a veritable bloodbath. More than forty people lost their lives and hundreds were wounded. The scenes on the television were hellish. The ground where the mosque had stood resembled a moonscape filled with black smoke, burned cars and glass panes that had been blown out of battered buildings. It felt awkward asking to look at the place where the tragedy occurred. I didn't want to come across as a morbid sight-seer, seeking the thrill of revisiting a disaster site. But Mohammed understood perfectly well that, as a journalist, I wanted to see a location that had important historical value.

After a long walk we arrived at the Al Salam mosque. The place was immaculate. The mosque itself basked in all its glory in the last rays of the setting sun, as if the horrific event of just a year before had never taken place. I was stunned by the speed and quality of the restoration. It was perfect. But when I turned my back to the mosque, the picture was quite different. The building opposite was still blackened and partly destroyed. We crossed the busy road so that I could take a photograph. As soon as I took my mobile phone out of my pocket, three men suddenly ran towards us out of nowhere. 'No photo!' they shouted and then switched over to Arabic. I realised straight away that we were in trouble. We were ordered to produce our identity papers, but it did not end there. The men motioned to us to follow them to an unspecified destination. They led us through an alley alongside the damaged building and into a tiny office of barely twelve square metres. One of the men, who wore a full black beard, took charge. He pointed to a leather sofa, and we silently seated ourselves. Taking his place behind a wooden desk, he began interrogating Elie and Mohammed. Another man took up position alongside a cabinet full of papers, and the third stood in front of the door, boldly blocking our exit.

I broke out in a cold sweat, not because of the heat, but because I feared that we would be interrogated separately. I hardly knew Mohammed and hoped that each of us would give these men the same account. We weren't going to be tortured, were we? The idea crossed my mind briefly. I feared the most for Mohammed. As a

Palestinian, he was the most vulnerable, as the Lebanese have no compassion for Palestinians. The men studied our identity cards thoroughly. Our interrogator took down our answers in a little notebook that had been passed on to him by his colleague next to the cabinet. There was no computer. The bearded man asked me in English where I was from and what my business was in Lebanon. I told him that I was a tourist and that we were on our way to the Corniche, which is the seafront boulevard. I considered for a moment calling the Dutch embassy, but then decided to wait and see. Despite Elie's excellent translating skills the men only partly understood my explanation. Fifteen minutes later, the interrogator had drawn his conclusion: we were harmless. They apologised profusely and the man who had stood guard at the door put his arm around my shoulder as a mark of friendship.

Once outside, I asked Elie what had happened, as most of the conversation had been in Arabic. My young friend explained that the head of the city's internal security had his residence opposite the mosque and that it was strictly forbidden to take pictures of it. As a resident of Trablous, Mohammed should have known that – at least according to the security guards.

Had Elie not been a Maronite, but Shiite or Alawi, we probably wouldn't have been released so quickly. We might even have been taken to another location for more thorough questioning. A rumour – unfounded – had spread that the Shiite group, Hezbollah, had been responsible for the 2013 bombing of the mosques.

As for me, I would have drawn the most suspicion, being a foreigner. What was a Dutch guy doing in this city that rarely attracted tourists? The bearded man had gone through my passport twice, searching for stamps of countries (such as Iran and Israel) that he considered to be enemies.

As we continued our walk, somewhat shaken by the encounter, the sun had finally set and there was the blasting of 'Allah-u-akbar' all around us. Despite our ordeal, the plan was still to visit a mosque, because Mohammed wanted to pray before breaking his fast. The mosque we had in mind was situated at the Corniche and is a somewhat smaller copy of the one at the Martyrs Square in central Beirut. Before he went in to pray, Mohammed washed his hands, face and feet. The imam, a kind man with a grey beard and a long white robe, nodded and smiled to welcome us. Other than Mohammed and the imam, there was no-one in the huge building. We were in conservative Tripoli, and it was Ramadan, so I was quite perplexed as to the conspicuous absence of the faithful in this house of prayer. Elie was as mystified as I was and chuckled. As far as he was concerned, the less religion there was, the better. He had already witnessed enough misery stemming from conflicting religious views in Lebanon.

When Mohammed had finished his prayers we took a shared taxi to *al-balad*, the centre of Trablous. Although we had been there earlier that day, the area was unrecognisable now with the crowds of people out to break their fast. Festive lights sparkled over the shopping street which was bursting with stalls selling food and drinks and other items. We found ourselves submerged in a seething and exuberant mass of revellers. I had seen nothing like this in Beirut. While Elie and I indulged in the hummus, falafel, haloum and sweet treats, sensible Mohammed ate moderately after his day of fasting.

When, at the end of the evening, we said goodbye to Mohammed, it felt as if I had known him forever. We hugged and kissed as if we had been lovers for years. This is typical in the Middle East, and so different from social relations in Europe. Our western habit of keeping new acquaintances at arm's length is quite baffling to Arabs: men in the Middle East are far more physical with each other than I am used to. (Straight) men hold hands and kiss one another on the cheek, even if they have only just met.

After a smooth ride back to Beirut, it turned out that our timing was perfect. When we got home Elie received a news alert from LBC News (the 'BBC' of Lebanon so to speak), reporting that just after midnight, the police had cordoned off the main roads to and from Trablous after violence had erupted in the city. Have I mentioned that you need a bit of luck when travelling through Lebanon?

XVI 'Jesus funeral'

Early in 2015 Elie urged me to come to Lebanon in time for Palm Sunday. I would see the famous processions on the Sunday before Easter. A very important event in Christian Lebanon, Elie had sent me photos from the previous year in which his nephews of four and six are seen waving their palm branches in front of an old church. Elie's light pressure was not enough to sway me. Although I would have enjoyed watching the procession, I didn't think it worth planning my trip around. For me personally, such an event has no particular religious significance. And if I really didn't want to miss such a celebration, I could have seen it in my home country, in Catholic Limburg or Brabant, for example. Therefore I stuck with my own plan and arrived in Beirut in the early morning of Maundy Thursday, the day Maronites visit seven churches (a reference to the first seven churches on the Seven Hills of Rome).

'Oh, not that mosque again!' I complained to Elie the day I arrived, when I was awoken after just a few hours napping on the couch in the living room. I said it with some astonishment because there was only one mosque in the neighbourhood, a Shiite one, and you normally only heard it during the call for prayer. Elie was enjoying the first day of the Easter holidays. Easter is a national holiday for the entire Lebanese population, including Muslims.

Playing with his smartphone as he always does in his spare time, Elie laughed at my ignorance. 'Come and look', he called, as he opened the French windows. From the balcony he pointed to the church diagonally below us. 'You think it's the imam, but actually it's a priest reading the letters of Jesus's disciples!' I was stunned. Noise levels like this would never be endured in a Dutch neighbourhood! Even with the windows and doors shut, it was as if the priest was standing right in the room. Elie explained that the ritual had begun on the previous Saturday evening and would come to an end only on Easter Sunday. While he spoke, I thought I heard the words 'Allah-u-akbar' (God is great) through the loudspeaker. I leaned further over the balustrade and asked Elie whether I had heard it correctly. He laughed out loud again. 'Now the Muslims hear it from the other side!' 'But is using the phrase Allah-u-akbar not reserved for Muslims only?' I asked Elie, who had begun (but not completed) training to be a priest. 'Allah just means God in Arabic. However, I have never heard Christians using that term. Perhaps you misheard, or maybe the priest made a mistake,' Elie was deadly serious and I assumed that it had just been my imagination. Blasting the words 'Allah-u-akbar' from a church's loudspeaker! That will be the day! Even in Lebanon.

The next day Elie invited me to come along to 'Jesus funeral', as he called the Good Friday Mass. At home I would have declined such an invitation but here in Lebanon I couldn't help being caught up in the Easter fever. A little after eleven o'clock, we took a shared taxi to the spot where the main road enters the neighbourhood of Ashrafieh, and then continued on foot towards the residence of the Maronite bishop of Beirut, a not-so-humble abode. As we approached, Elie joked about the bishop's belly that seemed to increase in size every year. Wide steps led us up to the basilica which was overflowing with people. The solid wood doors had been pushed wide open to allow the spring breeze inside. We placed ourselves discreetly at the back of the church and leaned against a pillar. The Mass was already in full swing and people were coming and going. It was so crowded that we had to keep squeezing against the pillar to allow people to pass. I heard children crying and parents reprimanding them. Congregants occasionally walked out of the church to have a chat with an acquaintance and then walked back in again.

The atmosphere was extremely laid back. How different this was from the Reformed Church in Rotterdam where my grandparents sometimes took me as a child: once the service had started, the doors would be closed, there would be absolute silence during the vicar's sermon and no-one in the congregation would dream of leaving the church except in an emergency!

Many female Lebanese churchgoers might not even be allowed into my grandparents' Reformed Church in Holland. Many of these women were dressed like Italian game show presenters: heavily made-up, hair bleached blonde, stiletto heels and clothes of the latest design that were just a little too provocative. These over-the-top fashion choices are considered appropriate during Easter, which represents a new beginning. The men too had put some effort into looking presentable with smart jackets and stylish shoes, but, being men, their style was more casual.

While I was listening to the Mass, I thought about the numerous attacks on mosques and churches in Baghdad that had left so many dead and a shiver ran down my spine. I looked around to see if there were any suspicious-looking characters about. Now and again when I am in Lebanon I have this overwhelming feeling of paranoia. How well was the security set up in this place? I didn't see anything to put my mind at rest, and nervous beads of sweat appeared on my forehead. There was some faint reassurance in the thought that the broad steps at the church entrance would offer us some protection from an exploding car bomb. But the thought I often have during precarious car journeys in the mountains came back to me: everyone has to die some time. Now is as good a time as any. My anxiety decreased when beautiful music in Aramaic (the language of Jesus) and Arabic filled the church. The hymns were reminiscent of Gregorian chants, but then in Arabic. The suffering of the Messiah, *their* Messiah, was palpable.

It ended with an actual burial of 'Jesus'. The head priest and two of his colleagues carried a black shroud through the church, followed by altar servers. After three rounds, the 'body' was laid in an ochre-yellow tent in a solemn moment. The congregation rose and walked up to it. Most people touched the tent's exterior briefly before making the sign of the cross. Many even took photographs. Elie en I joined in the procession past Christ's temporary resting place. It was only from right up close that I could see the golden cross on a stand in front of the closed opening of the tent.

The authenticity of the ritual was extraordinary. The tent became a tomb and people seemed to be genuinely grieving.

Two days later He would rise again. I felt completely immersed in this Bible story, even though I do not even consider myself a Christian.

It was only later, in the square in front of the church, when we ran into George, a friend of Elie's from a gay bar called Bardo, that I came back down to Earth. The two friends enquired after each other's families. The spell was broken.

'Come on, I've got something to show you', said Elie after we had said goodbye to George. In the same huge complex, there was another, somewhat smaller, church where the 'Jesus Funeral' was still in full swing. 'At three o'clock, both churches will start another Mass. They have to, because there is always so much demand for it', Elie said. Despite being a self-declared atheist, Elie took great pride in showing me these religious ceremonies. 'You in Europe, you can afford to stop going to church. If we follow your example in Lebanon it would be the end of Christianity here. That would make us a weak group and force us, in the end, to convert to Islam.' He said it without bitterness but the message was clear.

It's true that there once was a Christian majority in Lebanon. Officially, there still is, but only because the formal figures are based on a census from 1932. According to the statistics of the American intelligence agency, the CIA, at present only forty percent of the Lebanese population holds the Christian faith, contrasted with fifty-one percent in 1932. The Lebanese Information Centre estimates the figure even lower, at thirty-four percent, but this doesn't take into account the Palestinian and Syrian refugees. If it did, the proportion of Christians would fall spectacularly, as at least one in four inhabitants of Lebanon is a refugee. The 1932 census gives Lebanese Christians half of the seats in the Lebanese Parliament as well as the decree that the President has to be a Christian and, specifically, a Maronite. What would happen if the Syrians and other new groups obtained the right to vote? What would remain of Lebanon's Christian character?

On the evening of Good Friday the chanting from the loudspeaker of our neighbourhood church didn't cease at ten, as it had done the evening before, but kept going until eleven. Tofik, infuriated that the church had so forcefully intruded in his private space, spent the evening pacing and cursing. Elie said that the church would remain open the whole night as well as the following day, to give people the opportunity to pray for the salvation of the departed deity. Before I went to bed at about one that morning I glanced one last time at the church from the balcony. Churchgoers were still coming and going. The priest would not be alone tonight.

On Sunday I was woken by the triumphant and almost incessant chiming of church bells. No-one was permitted to ignore the resurrection of Jesus!

In the late afternoon the sound of drums and flutes filled the city, reminding me of Christmas in Beirut. The sun was shining gloriously and on the street I could see 'Bedouins' playing music and dancing. At least, that's what Elie had called them, but I later found out that they were actually Roma who live in the Beqaa Valley and travel to town on public holidays in the hope of earning some money. Today, they were in luck. Cheering residents threw coins from the balconies of the surrounding apartment blocks. Elie tried to teach me to say '*El Masih qam*' meaning 'The Messiah has Risen'. This was a complicated task, because the 'h' has a hard sound in Arabic. It is one of the sounds that is almost impossible to pronounce for non-Arabic speakers. You know that you are pronouncing it right when a mirror held in front of your face steams up when you say the word 'Masih'.

Easter, as I had never known it before, was at an end. Or so I thought. That same evening when Elie, Tofik and I sat relaxing on the balcony, Elie motioned for me to stand up. In the alleyway adjacent to the church with the loudspeakers I saw a long line of people approaching. A priest walked ahead and was followed by children. The adults were carrying lanterns. I was utterly confused.

Surely Easter was finished? When the procession neared us, I noticed that the children were carrying palm branches. It was the turn of the orthodox Lebanese Christians, who use a different calendar for Christmas and Easter. Exactly a week later, they too would chant '*El Masih qam*'.

XVII Spies

At the age of fifteen I went on an art class trip to Moscow. Talented teens from Rotterdam and Moscow were invited to collectively create a drawing to underline the bond of friendship between the Dutch and Russian people. This was in the days of Gorbachev and the Soviet Union. It was a thrilling adventure for us to pay a visit to the country we only knew from James Bond films: the land of spies. I vividly remember that my classmate, Arne, and I, as soon as we had been given the keys to the room we were sharing, proceeded to inspect behind the mirrors and under the mattresses and even took the light bulbs out of their fittings in search of listening devices and miniscule cameras. How disappointed we were when we didn't find anything.

There was, however, a spy in our midst. His name was Iwan and he was our travel guide. Although he had never been to the Netherlands, he spoke fluent Dutch. Everyone was convinced that his job was to keep a close watch on us, which was not very difficult as he could follow every word we schoolchildren were saying. The Russians seemed desperate not to let us 'escape' and admittedly, they did a good job because everything we did on that excursion, we did collectively and after we had arrived back in the hotel after a busy day, we were not allowed out until the next morning. When we left our rooms, we had to hand our key over to a 'warden' who was posted in the corridor and guarded our every move. At night, while in our room, Arne and I fantasised about how we would make our getaway (was Iwan listening through the hidden microphones?) But of course we knew that the Soviet apparatus would not in a million years let us get very far.

More than two decades after my Russian escapade, now in Lebanon, I couldn't help thinking about Iwan. Pavel, a young man in his late twenties, reminded me of him. He was working for a Polish institute and had rented a room at Elie's in the winter of 2014. Initially, there was nothing suspicious about Pavel. That was until Tariq, who occupied the room next to his, whispered to me that the Pole worked for the Israeli secret service, Mossad. I remember chuckling at this revelation. I told my travel companion, Linda, but of course she didn't know what to do with the information anymore than I did. After all, we had only arrived in Lebanon the previous day and had barely spoken to Pavel. Anyway, why would someone from Poland spy for the Israeli government?

In the house, the Mossad story seemed to be a running gag. When Elie passed Pavel in the corridor or anywhere else in the house he would whisper 'Mossaaaad...' over-pronouncing the word, and then disappear. Pavel laughed along with the joke, and then stared awkwardly at the ground. Even Tariq, who went to the gym with Pavel and had developed a friendship with him, kept half jokingly claiming that he was a spy.

The Mossad story roused my curiosity. When Elie returned from work the next day and we were alone in the kitchen, I decided to question him about Pavel. I simply couldn't believe the rumour. Neighbouring Israel was an enemy country and none of its inhabitants were permitted to cross the border into Lebanon. If caught, any spy from Israel risked a very long prison sentence.

Elie was willing to enlighten me on the condition that I kept my mouth shut. He added that he had promised Pavel not to tell anyone about him. It turned out that the young Pole had lived and worked in a kibbutz in Israel and had eventually converted to Judaism. So that was the big secret! That is why they teased him mercilessly by whispering 'Mossad'. I now sympathised with the shy young man from Poland.

Elie enjoyed being provocative. The rainbow flag on his balcony was proof of that. And if his friends had not prevented him, Elie would have bought an Israeli flag in the Shiite neighbourhood (where they sell American and Israeli flags to burn at demonstrations), and would have hung it proudly on the wall inside the house. At least, that's what he told me. The fact that supporting Israel is the biggest faux-pas one can make in Lebanon would normally appeal to Elie's rebellious nature, but even he could not bring himself to do this. Instead, he was an avid supporter of Judaism.

It is therefore unsurprising that it was Elie who came up with the idea to celebrate the Sabbath. He had convinced Pavel that it was safe for him to come out as a Jew. I made it easier for him by telling him about my own interest in Judaism and that I had visited Israel. Apart from our shared attraction to the religion, the young man and I had more in common. Pavel came from Krakow. I had Polish blood on my grandmother's side and had been to Krakow the previous summer. Before the Second World War, nearly a quarter of that city's inhabitants were Jewish. Only a small number of Polish Jews survived the concentration camps and many of them emigrated to Israel. Despite this, Krakow is still a charming city for visitors with an interest in its rich Jewish culture. Many of the synagogues still exist and have been beautifully restored, and the Jewish cemeteries are well looked after. Life in the Jewish quarter of Kazemier is starting to take off again and the number of Israeli restaurants in the city was striking. I told Pavel about my visit to the Community Centre where it appeared that more and more young Poles where rediscovering their Jewish roots. The Nazis had tried to annihilate the Jewish community in Poland, communism repressed the surviving Jews, but now Jewish life was cautiously being revived. Pavel was living proof of that.

The following Friday, just before sunset, we were ready for our Sabbath celebration. Pavel, who also had a Hebrew name but never used it in Lebanon, said the prayers, and Elie and I repeated after him. We were all wearing yarmulkes. Pavel already had his own and Linda had brought along two that she had obtained from the Portuguese synagogue in Amsterdam at Elie's request. Linda, Elie's sister and her friend observed the rite. We lit the candles, broke the bread and ate some of it. We had just made a toast ('l'chaim') and were about to drink the wine, when Tariq suddenly burst into the room, shouting 'Alaaaaha-u-akbar!' Everyone, including Pavel, laughed out loud. I didn't. I thought it was graceless and improper.

Meanwhile, I no longer believed that our Jewish friend was a spy. If Pavel really had been working for Mossad, he would never been so open about himself. The idea that this openness was precisely the cover-up he was using to allay suspicion seemed too far-fetched.

Yet, I do think there are a great many spies in Lebanon. It is a country that is used as a plaything by Russia and Iran on the one hand and the West and Saudi Arabia on the other. Before the Syrian civil war, President Assad's family was very influential in Lebanon. Today, the country is flooded with Syrian refugees, some of whom may hold valuable information about the Syrian regime, ISIS and other terror groups. And then, of course, there is neighbouring Israel which is regularly plagued by missile attacks launched from southern Lebanon.

At times I thought I had come across a spy. Tariq and I had a German acquaintance who seemed to be neither working nor studying. 'How does she have the money to stay here?' I asked Tariq. 'She is somehow able to rent a lovely studio, and she speaks Arabic fluently'. We then looked at one and another and exclaimed simultaneously: 'She's a spy!' But just as Arne and I could not find listening devices in the hotel in Russia, Tariq and I knew we had no proof.

All the same, you need to be vigilant in Lebanon when making jokes about spies. This became apparent during a New Year's Eve party in 2014. Just before Linda and I caught our flight home, we went out for a glass of champagne with Elie, Tofik and Pavel in the district of Hamra. Elie wanted to pay his friend Zena a visit. Zena lived in a stunning, elegantly furnished apartment. Every wall was decorated with her own artwork, including the walls of the toilet, which contained a chalkboard for visitors to comment on her creations. Zena was extremely generous with alcoholic drinks – the wine flowed and she even made us cocktails. Although it was December it was warm enough to sit in the garden, as long as we stayed out of the wind. We were introduced to her boyfriend who, with his three-piece suit and flamboyant moustache, looked as if he had materialised out of the nineteenth century, as well as two female friends who, judging from their clothes, probably came from well-to-do families. The atmosphere was exuberant. Somehow the conversation turned to Pavel: which part of Poland he was from and what he was doing in Beirut. On an impulse, Linda piped up: 'He works for Mossad.'

There was an uncomfortable silence. Pavel laughed nervously and Elie, leaping to his rescue said smilingly that, of course, that was a joke and slowly the buzz of conversation resumed. Elie signalled to me to accompany him a little way away from the rest of group. In a whisper, he informed me that the taciturn gentleman who seemed to have come from the nineteenth century belonged to a rich Shiite family. He urged me to tell Linda not to make such jokes again. In no time, Hezbollah could be knocking on the door to take Pavel away. Linda was mortified when I told her what Elie had just disclosed to me. She had obviously not meant any harm and was totally unaware that the sort of joke she had made was only suitable in the close domestic circle.

A little while later the night was filled with the sound of fireworks and the rattling of Kalashnikovs, the semi-automatic guns which Lebanese men shoot in the air on feast days. Luckily, this time I was at a safe distance from the Russian killing machines. The year before, as Elie and I had stood watching the New Year's fireworks from the balcony, Elie's downstairs neighbour had started shooting his Kalashnikov. Terrified, I dived into Elie's bedroom to get away as fast as I could.

Just after midnight Linda and I took a taxi to the airport. The cocktails and champagne lulled me into a deep sleep as soon as we boarded the aircraft. I dreamed that Pavel was locked in a dark cellar and bearded men were shining flashlights into the young Polish man's eyes. He admitted to them that he was Jewish, and a spy, after which they tortured him. I woke up as the plane was landing. Once on the ground, a stream of New Year wishes buzzed onto my phone. One of them was from my 'Mossad' friend. What a relief! I could breathe again. Pavel was safe.

XVIII Not allowed? Do it anyway!

Double-parking your car. Parking in a tunnel. Using your smartphone while driving. Having a couple of whiskies with Red Bull before you get behind the wheel. Cycling or jogging on the motorway. Driving at high speed around a blind corner while hoping there is no oncoming traffic... Of course these are all officially traffic offences in Lebanon, yet they are treated as optional advice by most Lebanese citizens. The law applies to *other* people as far as they are concerned. Anyway, if you are caught, it's easy to dodge the consequences, as long as you have money and good connections.

The 'do it anyway' attitude does not only apply to traffic offences. Take the animated nightlife in Beirut for example, which offers something for everyone. For instance, several bars and at least one nightclub are 'hook-up' spots only frequented by men. It is hard to tell how many of these establishments exist: you might hear about a bar that has just opened and then, when you are ready to try it a few months later, you find that it has already closed its doors. And then there is the delicate question how one determines whether it is a gay bar or not. At the Dunkin' Donuts in Hamra for example, mostly men can be seen sitting on the terrace which has a view over passersby. Of these men, all the gay stereotypes are represented: the older man with the pot belly and a small dog on his lap wearing a pink ribbon around its neck; the skinny young fashion queen; the workout guy straight from the gym and the one with a Mohawk and leather jacket (yes, even in the Middle East!). There is a lot of flirting and phone numbers are exchanged, but Dunkin' Donuts is obviously not a gay bar.

Hamra, which is situated in Muslim West Beirut, has a bar called Bardo, which is very popular among Beirut's gay community. My friend Linda, who herself is straight, was eager to see this famous location during her first visit to Lebanon. So, one Friday evening, Elie, Tariq and I took her along. Tariq parked his car right at the corner of the bar. It was midnight. At the entrance of the street where the bar was located, two soldiers kept watch. No traffic was allowed into the street without their permission. I saw my friend watching the guards. She was probably drawing a comparison with the Dutch Military Police who guard synagogues in Holland. To her surprise, she noticed the big bright letters spelling 'Bardo' on the front of the building. There was no official entrance and no security. A kind of garden path, that ran along a wall, led visitors to a back entrance. The path, which could be seen from the street, was overcrowded. Linda observed that almost all of the men were bearded, something she had noticed before. The sight of the male visitors also led her to conclude that the gyms in Lebanon must do good business. We lost Tariq almost immediately in the crowd. He had been going to Bardo nearly every night in the past few years. I joked that he practically lived there.

As we entered, we saw two women on the stage, dancing and kissing passionately. The small L-shaped bar had some space in the front and a dance floor at the back with tables and sofas. That's where we found Tariq again – he had gone in to arrange for a table to be freed up for us. Linda was bewildered as to how there could be gays dancing the night away here, while only a hundred kilometres away, the Muslim extremists of ISIS controlled the Lebanese town of Arsal at the eastern border. Couldn't something like that happen in Hamra? Weren't all these people, who were enjoying themselves without holding back, wrapped up in a false sense of security? Elie grinned at such a typically European observation. It was quite simple, he told her. As long as the bar owner paid the required bribe there would be no police raid.

Over the blare of the Lebanese pop music in the background, Linda asked Elie if he was ever afraid this club would be the target of a terror attack. I leaned in closer to hear his answer. My Lebanese friend said that terrorists had shown no interest in gay venues in his country. This reassured him that nothing would happen. Linda however remained unconvinced. 'If it's so safe, why is the army protecting Bardo?' she wanted to know. This amused Elie considerably. 'The soldiers aren't there for this bar! Further down the street is the residence of a politician!'

Linda asked me later whether, as someone who knew Lebanon, I shared Elie's confidence. She still needed reassurance. My reply was that, although I thought Elie was right, the situation could change at any moment. What was true today could make no sense tomorrow.

Take for example visitors to the al-Agha hammam, a Turkish bathhouse in Verdun in West Beirut. They thought they were safe. Then, on 9 August 2014, the police raided the hammam and arrested twenty-seven patrons for committing sexual acts that, under Article 534 of the Lebanese Penal Code, contradict 'the laws of nature'. The police did not actually catch anyone in the act but a tip-off that the hammam was being used as a gay cruising site was sufficient to justify the raid. According to media sources, all those arrested were Syrians, and included both visitors and staff members. It is completely plausible that any Lebanese men found in the bathhouse at the time of the raid were let off. Elie had heard that there was a priest among those arrested, but that he was released the next day after mediation by the church.

What happened at al-Agha is not an isolated incident. Some of the obscure rundown cinemas in Beirut that cater only to men have also, in recent years, been the target of police raids. Interestingly enough, as with the hammams, some of the cinemas seem to be off the police radar, which suggests that bribes and high-level connections determine which locations can guarantee the safety of their patrons and which cannot.

Article 534, the law that forbids 'unnatural' sexual behaviour, is the one that strikes fear in the heart of every gay Lebanese person. Breaking the law can cost the offender a year in prison and a fine. In January 2014, a Lebanese judge deemed that a transgender woman having a relationship with a man was not punishable under Article 534. Theoretically, this should have been a huge breakthrough for the Lebanese gay community. Unfortunately, there is no real reason for optimism. Already in 2009, Justice Mounier Sleiman had ruled that sexual relations between two people of the same sex did not necessarily constitute 'unnatural sex' and yet homosexuals are still prosecuted under Article 534. Moreover, the Association of Lebanese Physicians ruled in 2012 that doctors were no longer permitted to participate in anal examinations on gay men that were conducted by the police. These intrusive and humiliating tests were performed in order to determine whether anal sex had taken place, even though the doctor's association admitted that the tests were inconclusive. In spite of being forbidden since 2012, reports of this method being employed by police were still being made after that date. However, it should be stated in the 2018 edition of this book that this appalling practice seemed to have ceased.

Is the situation improving for LGBTQI people? I doubt it. I recently spoke to a 28 year-old man who was caught red-handed. He was in a car park kissing his boyfriend in the car when he was accosted by the police. He was willing to share his story on the condition of anonymity. He told me that after his arrest, he was interrogated several times by the police and made to appear before the court. He had had to lie to his family and employer (both unaware of his sexual orientation), and lived in fear they would discover that he had stood trial. Although, like the judge, he is a Christian, this did not help him in the slightest. 'She showed no sympathy for the LGBTQI cause at all. She made it clear that she was disgusted by it. And most importantly, she did not follow the precedent of other judges.' Her verdict was two months imprisonment, but he was set free on probation. 'If I'm ever caught again, I'll immediately end up in jail.' I remarked that he had had a lucky escape but he did not agree. 'Till today that episode has ruined my life. I spent my savings on my lawyer, I live in constant fear of anyone discovering my secret and I am petrified of being caught again. The stress is unbearable.'

To have Article 534 scrapped would be a blessing for the LGBTQI community. It would free them from the risk of being prosecuted. Sadly, this is not likely to happen anytime soon: conservatives from both the Islamic and Christian sides will use their powerful position to thwart a change in the law.

A poll has revealed that a fifth of the Lebanese population believes that homosexuality should be legalised (Pew Research, 2014). This result means that, in the region, only Israel precedes Lebanon as liberal champion. Yet, the reality is that eighty percent of the country is still against LGBTQI rights. Hence, only a small number of well-known Lebanese LGBTQI has had the courage to come out of the closet. Elie and I once interviewed a famous Lebanese actress. She is a Christian and is known to be open-minded. The interview was to be published in the magazine of an LGBTQI organisation called Helem. But just before it could take place, the actress got cold feet. She explained that the timing was too risky for her. She was waiting to hear back about possible new acting roles and the Church had a lot of influence in the selection process. Hopefully we would understand? Regretfully, she had to decline the interview, even though in the restaurant she was plainly surrounded by friends from the gay community.

Nevertheless, there are also examples of great courage. The lead singer of the group Mashrou' Leila (A Nocturnal Project), the most successful Lebanese band in recent years, makes no secret of his sexual orientation. His name is Hamed Sinno and he doesn't hesitate to fly the rainbow flag during performances. He did this during the Byblos Festival in 2010, an event which was attended by the Lebanese Prime Minister. In 2013 he appeared on the cover of the French LGBTQI magazine, Têtu.

When Mashrou' Leila scheduled a concert in the predominantly Christian town of Zouk Mikael in the summer of 2013, there was fierce opposition among the town's population. They made their reason crystal clear; they didn't want to have that 'faggot' in their town. Facebook pages were launched opposing the performance and politicians were put under pressure, but the organisers of the event persisted. They could not risk cancelling the Mashrou' Leila act, their biggest crowd-puller.

During their Easter show in the One Beirut concert hall in 2015, there was an unexpected turn of events. Sinno sang one of his numbers about lost love. The song, called 'the scent of jasmine', is about a woman, or so it seemed from his use of masculine pronouns like 'he' and 'his' as is customary in traditional Arabic poetry. This sounded odd coming from the lips of the openly gay singer. But when he started changing the lyrics to say that he wanted to be the wife of the other man in the song, the crowd lost control. Ten thousand young Mashrou' Leila fans cheered hysterically. It was a sign of hope. In July 2018 The Lebanese Court of Appeals ruled that homosexuality is not a crime. A major milestone for the Lebanese LGBTQI community. Maybe, just maybe, things will change in Lebanon.

IX Elie in trouble

Elie was oblivious to danger and lived his life without restraint. When friends warned him about the risk of flying a rainbow flag from his balcony he would shrug his shoulders. 'Nobody here knows it's the gay flag', he would say. He was not afraid of going out on the street wearing earrings and a pink t-shirt and carrying a backpack with buttons pinned onto it which read 'I love sex' or 'I love men'. As far as he was concerned, anything was possible in Lebanon. Unfortunately, as it turned out, he was too naïve. I would not go as far as saying that Elie was as prominent as the American activist, Harvey Milk, but the two men did share a fighting spirit. Elie once took part in a march through Beirut, protesting the country's anti-gay laws. This tiny demonstration, which counted barely thirty participants, he referred to as the Beirut Gay Pride. The pictures that were taken that day still appear today in newspapers and magazines concerned with gay rights in the Middle East, given the rarity of relevant visuals to accompany these articles. Such protest marches in Jordan, Syria or Egypt would be unthinkable, while in Saudi Arabia, protesters would probably be given the death sentence.

Naturally, Elie was also present for the International Day against Homophobia held on 17 May 2015 in the Monroe Hotel in Beirut. Shortly after the event, he was interviewed by the Lebanese national broadcaster, LBC. That same evening, viewers saw for the first time on television someone who said that there was nothing wrong with being gay and that it was about time for society to accept homosexuality. Elie was the only one of the interviewees who was clearly recognisable on the screen. His first and last names were also displayed.

The next day Elie noticed that he was attracting blatant looks of disapproval on the street. Most of his co-workers, scandalised by his life choices, condemned him, while others surreptitiously commended him for his bravery. That evening, Elie's brother-in-law telephoned, fuming with rage. He accused Elie of bringing shame on him and his family, and warned him that if he didn't change his ways there would be consequences. It was an unconcealed threat.

A month after the interview, on 18 June to be exact, Elie came home from work to find a hand-written note in Arabic taped to his door. Referring to the television interview, the anonymous writer informed Elie that he would burn in hell and ordered him to find another place to live if he wanted to stay in one piece. Elie sent me a photo of the threatening letter. Was this a sick joke by a neighbour or a jealous ex-boyfriend? Was his brother-in-law behind it? Or was it far more serious? Perhaps an ISIS or Al Nusra supporter had been able to trace him? Of course I had no way of knowing but I urged Elie to be very careful and not to leave his house alone anymore. I was haunted by the reports out of Bangladesh, where anyone who dares to go against the strict Islamic laws is brutally murdered, often with a machete. Could it be that Lebanon awaited the same fate?

I tried to persuade Elie to report the threats to the police and to get himself a lawyer. But he was convinced that the police would turn on him, instead of on the people who were threatening him. I feared that he might be right.

A week later, on 26 June, another note was stuck on Elie's door. This time the threat was more acute. 'You ignored the warning, now you can choose: beat it now, we will deal with you outside, when you are alone and least expect it. Then you will bleed for what you have done.'

The moment had come for Elie to go into hiding. My young Lebanese friend moved from his flat back to his parents' home. His parents were a little surprised to find him on the doorstep of their cramped two-room apartment which they already shared with their other two adult children. But Elie did not explain about the threats he had received. His parents were both heart patients and he thought the news might kill them.

On 9 July Elie's mother found the third threatening letter. It was stuck to her front door and addressed to her son. 'There is no use in hiding. We will find you anywhere you go.' It was at that moment that I knew that Elie's life was really in danger and that he had to leave Beirut. In a panic, Elie moved to a secret address on the outskirts of Beirut. He made contact with Mosaic, an organisation funded by international donors which gives advice and assistance to sexual minorities in Lebanon. The organisation told Elie point blank to leave the country: they could not help him anymore.

I couldn't believe it had come to this. Elie's parents had stayed in Lebanon during a bloody civil war because of their loyalty to their country and now Elie was going to leave because of these threats? I had hoped he would fight back, just as Harvey Milk, the San Francisco city councillor, had, back in the 1970s. But it was easy for me to say, safely tucked away in the Netherlands. How would I react if I were threatened by an invisible enemy?

Before he started receiving the threatening letters, Elie had applied for a tourist visa in the Netherlands, as he had done the year before. Unfortunately, the visa would only be valid three weeks later. I would not forgive myself if something happened to him in the meantime. We decided that Istanbul was the best place for him to hide out temporarily, as Lebanese citizens are allowed to travel to Turkey without a visa.

The Elie I encountered in Istanbul was unrecognisable. The dreadful events at home had traumatised him and he looked permanently frightened and pale. He hardly went out, ate almost nothing and was afraid of being attacked, even in Istanbul. As we walked together along the Istiklal, a shopping street in the European part of the city, Elie confided in me that he wanted to apply for asylum in the Netherlands. It was a heart-wrenching decision. He would be separated from his life partner, Tofik, for a long time. It dawned on me that he would also be subjected to abuse that was often inflicted on gay men by radical Muslims in Dutch asylum seeker centres, and at that moment, I decided that Elie would move in with me while his application was being processed. And so, Elie made his way to the Netherlands in July 2015.

A year later, in July 2016, Elie moved for the second time; this time from my house to his own studio in Amsterdam. His partner was only able to join him one year later, due to very slow family reunion procedures.

Many people with dissenting opinions, dissenting religions as well as gays, lesbians and transsexuals have found refuge in Europe. It is an exodus from the Middle East that will, unfortunately, not come to an end any time soon.

Epilogue

What has become of the people in this book? How are they getting on, two years after our first publication? And what is the situation in Lebanon like now?

In August 2015, Elie arrived in the Netherlands on a tourist visa. His application to be recognised as a refugee took one year. I spared him staying in an asylum-seeker centre, where he might have faced anti-gay behaviour or even violence. I gave him his own room in my house in The Hague, just as a year full of anxiety was beginning for him. Although he had a strong story and was sure he would be granted refugee status, he was a different Elie to the one I had known in Lebanon: fretful, pining for his partner, Tofik, and for his family, he escaped his worries by smoking joints and partying. One good initiative was that my friend immediately got involved with the Amsterdam-based Secret Garden, a foundation that helps refugees who are gay, lesbian, transgender, queer or confused about their sexuality. This voluntary job was perfect for him. He organised meetings about the danger of HIV/Aids, self-awareness and many other issues that concern migrants coming from countries like Syria, Iraq and Pakistan. He also got involved in organising the International Migrant Queer Film festival. I have to say I was, and am, very proud of his contributions to Dutch society.

Everything changed personally for Elie when his partner joined him in the Netherlands. I watched the tears stream from their eyes when they finally found each other again at Schiphol airport in the summer of 2017. After living together for more than six months in a tiny studio in a remote district of Amsterdam (Bijlmermeer), they moved this year to a bigger house near the centrally-located

Vondelpark. In two years, Elie will be eligible for Dutch citizenship and then he can return to Lebanon to see his parents, who miss him terribly. I can say it has been a journey full of sacrifices for them.

Rabih, Elie's friend who drove us through the Kadisha Valley, is living his dream. After finishing his financial studies in Beirut and working for a while, he lived in Paris and London and will soon go to Shanghai.

Sam, co-owner of Recycle Beirut, is still going strong. His business is growing and more and more companies and institutions are working with him and his American business partner. Amazingly, he still has another job alongside Recycle Beirut. Sam recently travelled for the first time, which is much harder for him as a Palestinian than it is for Lebanese citizens. He was in Sri Lanka for a recycling project and toured Europe extensively last year.

Tariq, who showed me around the city of Sour, also moved to Ashrafieh. He lives in a big, well-furnished rental apartment and rents two of his three rooms out to foreigners. He, too, recently travelled abroad for the first time.

My friend Linda, who had never wanted to go to Lebanon, kept going back. She fell in love with the people, who reminded her so much of her beloved island of Crete. She is in contact, almost on a daily basis, with her Lebanese friends and in her house I often hear Lebanese music playing.

Ronnie Chatah has resumed his guided city tours. After his father was assassinated in 2013 he immediately stopped the tours and stayed in the United Kingdom for a while. I do not know him personally, but I think it is a good sign for Lebanon that people like Ronnie return there.

Another good sign was that Lebanon deftly handled a severe political crisis that could have led to violence or even war in the fall of 2017. I am referring to the resignation of Prime Minister Saad Hariri while he was in Saudi Arabia in November 2017. It was world news, because after his resignation, Hariri did not return to Lebanon. According to President Michel Aoun, the Prime Minister was not free in Riyaad and was de facto being held hostage by the Saudis. It was only after the intervention of French President Macron that Hariri left Riyaad eleven days after his resignation speech. First to Paris, then following a visit to Cairo, he arrived in Beirut four days later. Once in the Lebanese capital he put his resignation – which had not been accepted by the President as long as he was not in Lebanon – on hold. He resumed office on December 5 and things appeared to go back to normal in Lebanon.

Looking back, this had been one of the most bizarre episodes in post-war Lebanese history. Saad Hariri had harshly criticised his coalition partner, Hezbollah, in his resignation speech in Saudi Arabia. The Saudi crown prince even added that they considered their kingdom to be at war with Lebanon! His logic was that, since a rocket from Yemen had hit the airport of Ryaad and the rebels in Yemen were supported by Hezbollah, Lebanon had declared war on Saudi Arabia. Tension was high in the nation. Added to this, Israel was giving signals that the whole of Lebanon would be a target in the next war with Hezbollah, not just the Shiite militia itself. Since Israel and Saudi Arabia opened diplomatic channels some time ago, joint military action against Lebanon was not deemed impossible either.

Hezbollah's reaction to all of this was limited to words. When Saad Hariri was in Ryaad, the party said it wanted the Prime Minister of Lebanon to return as soon as possible. Leader Hassan

Nasrallah stressed that Hariri was also their Prime Minister. President Aoun, an ally of Hezbollah, followed the same line. And then Sunni people started to go out into the street in Tripoli, demanding Hariri's return. During the Beirut Marathon, the image of Hariri was everywhere. Ironically, the strange events in Ryaad ultimately resulted in harmony between Shiites, Christians and Sunni Muslims. This was unprecedented in Lebanon and saved the country from disaster.

Am I positive about Lebanon's future? I wish with all my heart that I could shout from the rooftops that I am. The unity displayed around Hariri's 'resignation' is a cause for hope. But the words of Thomas E. Friedman stay in my mind, when he wrote in his great work, *From Beirut to Jerusalem*: in the Middle East you do not eat just the egg, you eat it with the shell. So you will leave nothing for your enemies.

As a witness of the Lebanese Civil War, Friedman believed this was the leitmotif for all leaders in the region. Therefore, unity between sects might be a *fata morgana*, a mirage. But then again, it might not, because history does not always repeat itself. Things can change. Let's hope the moment of change will soon come for Lebanon and that it will be irreversible.

Lebanon, may peace be upon your people!

Martijn van der Kooij
Beirut, February 7, 2018

Things to do & my own favourite places

Lebanon

Transportation

Though the country is small, it feels big because of the mountain chain separating the coastal areas from inland. There are almost always traffic jams on most of the highways in the Beirut area, so it will take you longer than expected to get from A to B. Driving is only advisable if you are a very experienced driver. There are basically no rules on the road and at night many people ignore traffic lights. Getting around by **minibus** or **minivan** (small buses that carry 15 or 30 passengers) is a solution: they are cheap and can take you anywhere. (**Shared**) **taxis** can also be found everywhere and are very affordable. They are called '**service**' (pronounced 'ser-*vees*') and usually use old cars. You can recognise them by their red number plate; there is no taxi sign or taxi company name. When the car stops, you just shout the destination to the driver (do not bother to say hello). He will either gesture for you to get in or quickly drive away without saying anything. Do not be offended. The rate is fixed: inside Beirut 2000 LL (1.30 USD) for a short trip and 4000 LL for a long one. In Trablous (Tripoli) and Sour (Tyre) you will pay only 1000 LL/2000 LL. For trips outside of the city you need to negotiate the price. If the driver asks '*serviceen*' (the plural of *service*), it means he wants to be paid double. You can negotiate and say, if it's reasonable, 'service o noos' (one and a half service). It's fair to pay a bit more late at night.

I have had very good experiences with **Uber** in Beirut. Simply download the app. You can pay cash if you like.

Safety

Crime rates are low in Lebanon and street crime, such as robbery, is very rare. There are pickpockets, but only in crowded places like the flea market. In contrast with Egypt, for example, there is hardly any **harassment of women** in public places. Women are never obliged to cover their heads, except when entering a mosque. In general, Lebanese people dress very well. Be aware that the dress code is modest in the more conservative areas. This is especially the case in the Sunni cities of **Tripoli**, **Akkar** and **Sidon** and to a lesser extent in **Tyre** and **Baalbek**.

Always check the latest news on Lebanon and your embassy's warnings before travelling. The security situation is generally good, but this can change rapidly. As long as the war in Syria continues, it's not a good idea to spend time in the border area.

Do you want to play it safe? Visit the popular neighbourhoods in Beirut (**Hamra**, **Monot**, **Badaro**, **Gemmayze**, **Mar Mikhael**, **Ashrafieh**) and the Christian towns on the coast between the capital and Tripoli (**Byblos**, **Jounieh**, **Anfeh**). The **Khadisha Valley**, as well as being one of the most beautiful places in the country, is also safe. The risk of sudden violence or attacks is low in all of these areas.

The opposite is true for the mainly Shiite settlement of **Dahieh** in South Beirut. This Hezbollah-controlled suburb, which has been hit many times by car bombs and was shelled by Israel in the 2016 war, is avoided even by many Lebanese people.

The **Palestinian refugee camps** in Lebanon have a very bad reputation and even the police do not venture into them. Think twice before you go, or visit them with a local whom you trust. They are compelling for sure, with their narrow, winding streets and portraits of Yasser Arafat everywhere. The **Ain al-Hilweh** camp, close to Sidon, is known to be a hideout for wanted Islamic extremists. It has one of the worst (but still not *the* worst) reputations of all the camps.

Beirut

The Lebanese capital used to be known as the 'Paris of the Middle East', but this term is misleading for present-day Beirut. While there is definitely a French influence in the architecture, the city won't remind you much of Paris, unless you are downtown at the **Place de l'Étoile** (or El Nejmeh), where the name speaks for itself. In this area, some of the grandeur of the French capital can be discerned, but on a smaller scale. More prevalent are the old villas from the Ottoman period that can still be found in **Mar Nicolas** (for example the one that houses the **Sursock Museum**). Some of the streets have kept their traditional character, including **Gemmayze Street** and the meandering streets of the **Geitawi** area. For trendy, modern architecture, visit **Zeituna Bay**, which has become one of the fanciest parts of town.

In terms of its nightlife, Beirut outdoes Paris. In fact, Beirut is far ahead of most cities in the world in this regard. Restaurants start getting full between nine and ten and even at midnight you can be served almost everywhere. Many bars and clubs are open until the early hours, especially at the weekend. I have listed some of my favourite places below.

Parks are rare. Most Beirutis get their share of sports and exercise at the **Corniche**, the road that runs along the coast for several kilometres. The city's only beach is **Ramleh** Beach – not a bad place to lie down and relax for a while. With high buildings behind you, green mountains and blue sea water, you might suddenly think you are in Rio the Janeiro. Swimming is a different matter. Not only can there be strong currents, but, this close to the city, the water may be polluted. It's better not to take the risk if in doubt!

Must see

- The **Sursock Museum**: In the residence of Nicolas Sursock, one of the richest Lebanese men in the 19th century, you will find modern, mostly European art. It is a fine collection that is part of 5000 pieces that Nicolas Sursock collected during his lifetime. This is an extremely well-maintained museum. Entrance is free. It is open every day except Tuesday from 10.00 to 18.00 and on Thursdays until 21.00. www.sursock.museum

- **National Museum** – Known as Mathaaf. Concrete walls were raised around the ancient statues and tombs during the Civil War, and thanks to these the collection was saved. It's a small museum, but it contains many precious objects from the Bronze Age up until the Mamaluk era. It's open from 9.00 to 17.00 from Tuesday to Sunday, closed during holidays. After your visit to the National Museum, take a walk down **Badaro Street**, the most European-style street in Lebanon, featuring some excellent bars and restaurants. www.beirutnationalmuseum.com

- **Bourj Hammoud** – On Saturdays, dive into the craziness of this Armenian Quarter, with its many small, cheap shops and continuous traffic jams. Bourj Hammoud is known to be a good place to buy jewellery. To get here, follow Armenia Street away from downtown, and cross the bridge over the Beirut river. After five minutes you will arrive at **Municipality Square**. The café in the middle of the square is a nice place to drink tea, coffee or freshly squeezed orange juice. Opposite Byblos Bank, on the other side of the square, you will see a small bakery (**Bash Mankoush**) which serves delicious flat breads, mini-pizzas and much more. You can take your food to eat at the above-mentioned café.

Armenians specialise in handicrafts. If you don't mind walking a bit more, follow Mar Youssef Street, which is right off SGBL Bank on Municipality Square. If you are crazy about *fool* (beans!), hummus and fresh vegetables you have two options in this street: the popular **Abou Hassan** or the more elegant restaurant, **El Hana**, opposite it. At the end of the street you will see a **monument** for the Armenian Genocide. Was it deliberately made to be unattractive because of what it represents? Decide for yourself. If you are still hungry, take a right at the corner of the Total petrol station, into Maggie el Hajj Street. Within five minutes you will see the **Moses Bakery** on the left side of the street, an Armenian family business that offers the best pizzas in town! This bakery closes around 16.00.

• **Saint George Greek Orthodox Cathedral and Church** The cathedral is on the Place de l'Étoile, opposite the Parliament building and the church lies in the street of Saint George Orthodox Hospital (also called Roum Hospital). In addition to all the hand-painted frescos and elaborate icons in both churches, the Cathedral includes an underground museum where you can see the roman foundations on which it was built. It is a small museum, but very well put together. Entrance for the archaeological museum costs 5000 LL. The second church is more spectacular with its extravagant use of gold plate. It's a relatively new building – from 2007 – but it feels like it has always been there.

- **Mohammed al-Amin Mosque/ 'The Blue Mosque'**

Like the church above, it looks like this mosque has always stood here, but it's actually a new building (from 2005). Before the Civil War this part of the Martyrs Square was a prayer corner. After the War, this grand Sunni mosque was built on the initiative of Rafiq Hariri. Visitors are very welcome to admire the splendour of this religious monument. The carpets, crystal chandeliers, painted texts from the Quran and the carved wood together leave a very striking impression. During prayer times the mosque is closed to non-Muslims. Be aware that on Fridays, a holy day for Muslims, the place is not open to female tourists. Opening times are from sunrise to sunset.

- **Souq al-Ahad** – The Sunday market that is also open on Saturdays. If you're looking for a bargain, this is the place to head. There are second-hand shops where, for a few dollars you can get hold of Arabic-style old lamps, boxes and even sometimes beautiful old doors. You might not want to take a door home with you, but they are definitely worth looking at. The souq is located at Sin el Fil near Beirut Art Centre; any taxi driver will know how to find it. Bus 15 (1000 LL) stops at the souq. Open from 9.00 to 18.00.

- **Hamra Street** Stroll down Hamra Street if you are looking for (souvenir) shops, restaurants and (coffee) bars. At night it gets very busy. If you are coming from the city centre you can take a right turn and visit the famous American University of Beirut (take your passport with you, sometimes you need it to enter). It's a big, beautiful 19th century complex that includes tennis courts, swimming pools, and sports halls. This is the most prestigious university in Lebanon.

City walks

• **Be Beirut** A highly recommended tour by experienced guide, Ronnie Chatah (see chapter XI) who will give you a lively and humorous rundown of Beirut's history. www.bebeirut.org

Beirut Free Walking Tour: a new concept, introduced in 2018 in Beirut. Meet in downtown Beirut and tip the guide as much as you like after the tour. Find 'Beirut Free Walking Tour' on Facebook for up-to-date information.

Bars and restaurants

• **Bar360 Le Gray Hotel**, at Martyrs Square next to the Virgin Store. The rooftop terrace, open all year except in the winter, offers a stunning view over the city, with the Blue Mosque and the Maronite Cathedral in the spotlight. On clear winter days you can try the terrace one floor below which gives you an impressive view of the Martyrs Square and even features a small swimming pool. For people travelling on a small budget, however, this is not the best option.

• **Badguer**, Melkonian Street. Look for the pink building on the corner (almost at the end of the street going towards the river).

This Armenian restaurant and community centre offers excellent food. Try the cherry kebab with Aleppo cherries, the *itch* (Armenian salad) or the *soubarak* (three sorts of cheese between layers of paper-thin pastry). The meaty grilled aubergine is aubergine at its best! Affordable prices. *www.badguer.com*

• **Enab**, Armenia Street in the Geara Building. Apart from the excellent *mezzes* (Arab 'amuse-bouches') and specialities which include frog legs and small birds, the setting is perfect for long dining on its large and very pleasant terrace. Mid-range prices. www.facebook.com/Enabbeirut

• **Em Nazih, Rue Pasteur in Gemmayze.** Take the steps down next to Lodge or enter from the Charlie Helou bus station. This is one of the nicest places in town to eat *mezzes* with friends, have a few drinks and play backgammon or pool. Also a good place for those who like *aiguilles* (water pipes). Friendly staff and a diverse crowd. On Friday and Saturday nights there is live music. It has a small but inviting outside terrace. www.saifigardens.com/en/cafe

• **Em Nazih, Hamra.** Pretty much the same as the one in Gemmayze, but much smaller. www.saifigardens.com/en/cafe

- **Snack Garo,** next to Malaab (the football stadium) in Bourj Hammoud at Masaken Road, is a popular sandwich shop that offers a great variety of delicious fast food (sandwiches, fried potatoes, salads). If you are around: go for it!

- **Coop d'état,** Rue Pasteur in Gemmayze. Go down the steps, enter the main hall of Saifi Urban Gardens (just before Em Nazih), climb to the upper floor and you will find this rooftop bar. Especially enjoyable on warm summer days, when Coop d'état turns into a beach hut, with sand on the floor and a miniscule plastic pool. Most people wear beach clothes.

- **Urbanista,** Rue Gouraud (Coming from the direction of downtown it is near the beginning of the road, on the left). A modern, friendly place which serves excellent coffee. It has a small terrace in the back.

- **T-Marboota,** on Hamra Street, is not easy to find, but keep in mind it's on the same square as Starbucks on Hamra Street. On the opposite corner of the square, a door will lead you to T-Marboota. Eat wonderful *mezzes* on the terrace and strike up a conversation with other customers.

• **Mezyan**, on Hamra Street, offers great *mezzes* and is a popular dancing venue later at night. Coming from downtown it's located on the right between Costa Café and Starbucks. As usual it's a bit hidden: to find the entrance, turn right after BLC Bank into the small alleyway.

Where to stay

• **Mady's hostel**, Gemmayze. By chance I discovered this small, friendly hostel with only three private double rooms, two shared bathrooms, a living room and kitchen. You can enjoy your breakfast on the large balcony of this early 20th century building. It is very clean and affordable (around $30 per night). You can arrange to be picked up at the airport. There is no generator, so you will have to deal with three hour-long power cuts on a daily basis: if you can survive for a few hours without wifi, air-conditioning and a lift, it is a great place to stay. www.madyshostel.com

• **Saifi Urban Gardens**, Rue Pasteur. Take the steps down by the Lodge. This is a cheaper option in Beirut and next to Em Nazih. There are (basic) shared or private rooms. Many young international people stay here. www.saifigardens.com

• **Airbnb** offers some wonderful options to stay in typical 19th century Lebanese houses. www.airbnb.nl

Outside Beirut

Hiking

• **Lebanon Mountain Trail**

The Lebanon Mountain Trail (LMT) is the first long-distance hiking trail in Lebanon. It extends from Andqet in the north of Lebanon to Marjaayoun in the south: a 470 km (293 mile) path that runs through more than 75 towns and villages at altitudes ranging from 570 meters to 2,011 meters (about 1,840 to 6,000 feet) above sea level. 'The LMT showcases the natural beauty and cultural wealth of Lebanon's mountains and demonstrates the determination of the people of Lebanon to conserve this unique heritage. The trail brings communities closer together and expands economic opportunities in rural areas through environmentally- and socially-responsible tourism', according to the organisation's website.

In order to promote the trail, the LMT organises two hiking trips per year, the Thru Walk in April and the Fall Trek in October. If you want to do the walk in another period, you can hire a local tour guide. **Never hike alone.** www.lebanontrail.org

Skiing

• Lebanon is the only country in the Middle East which has facilities for outdoor skiing. Since I dislike snow and cold weather, I have never been to a ski resort, but if you are a fan you can ski your heart out in Lebanon. The country has six resorts of which Mzaar Kfardebian is the biggest. Most resorts are a little over one hour's drive from Beirut. wikitravel.org/en/Skiing_in_Lebanon

Visiting wineries

• Lebanon has a long history of making wine. There is evidence the first grapes were harvested around 5000 B.C by the Phoenicians. The Lebanese climate offers excellent conditions for making wine. Most of the present day wineries have their vineyards in the southern Beqaa Valley. Chateau Ksara is by far the biggest. Second in place is Château Kefraya. Both wineries offer tours to visitors on a daily basis. The many small and more exclusive Lebanese winemakers can be visited on appointment, though during the harvest season they might be too busy. Guided 'wine tours are organised a few times a year by Camille Karout, who imports the most refined Lebanese wines from Lebanon to Belgium and the Netherlands. Info: gopicbvba@gmail.com (+31 (0) 684960035

Byblos (Jbeil)

'Wow, this looks like Malta', a friend of mine once said when he saw the old harbour of Byblos. Jbeil, as it is called locally, is definitely the closest you can get to Europe: 'Lebanon-light'. Where else can you find such a well-kept, clean and modern city in Lebanon? (Actually, I later learned that some Christian and Druze mountain villages are even more impeccable). The predominantly Christian town of Jbeil is good for dining out, but be prepared to pay higher prices. It's also good for a night out on the terraces of the many pubs in the **restored souq**. And of course there are archaeological sites (the **Mamaluk castle, port** and remnants of (**pre-)Phoenician foundations** are the main attractions). It's believed to be one of the oldest human settlements in the world and the old part of town is UNESCO World Heritage.

In the summer the city is usually swarming with tourists and it can be extremely hot. **Christmastime** is special because the old part of town is decorated flamboyantly (read my story in chapter X and see the pictures on page 88). Many Lebanese people flock to Jbeil to marvel at the spectacle. A Christmas experience in the Middle East does not get more special than this!

Also unmissable is a visit to the **John the Baptist church**, which dates back to 1115 AD. The serene atmosphere in this church is of indescribable beauty.

To **get to Jbeil** from Beirut is very easy: Take any bus from the Doura roundabout in front of Byblos Bank in Beirut. With no traffic jams (unlikely during day time) it takes 30 minutes. There are also direct buses from the Cola and Charles Helou Bus Stations. Ask the driver to stop at 'Bou Khalil supermarket', go down and take the tunnel under the highway. On the way back you can wait on the other side of the highway where there are usually buses waiting to take you back to Doura (1500 LL, one way).

Mar Maroun Monastery

You can easily combine your trip to Byblos with a spiritual detour into the mountains. About a half-hour drive from the port town, lies the monastery of Mar Maroun in **Annaya**. This is where the most iconic saint of Lebanon: **Mar (Saint) Charbel** (1877-1922) lived. He is said to have cured sick people and Lebanese people go to the monastery to pray for the recovery of their loved ones. Many Lebanese men are named after Charbel, which makes it, together with Elie, the most common name among male Christians. The small museum nearby shows visitors how the Saint used to live. www.saintcharbel-annaya.com

You can reach the monastery by **private taxi** from Byblos (around $25-30 for a round trip).

TIP: Visit **Jeita Grotto** (the famous and most beautiful caves in the world) in the morning, tour **Byblos** in the afternoon and end the day at **Mar Maroun Monastery**. If you wake up early, your itinerary can also include taking the **Téléférique** (Cable tram) from Jounieh to Harissa, where you can admire Beirut and the sea from a colossal Virgin Mary statue (**The Lady of Harissa**).

Batroun (beach life)

From the Seaside Road you go down the steps next to the old and rusty lift. Here you will find **Pierre and Friends** – beach life at its best! The beds are almost in the sea and the clean, warm water makes swimming conditions perfect. Pierre and Friends serves excellent (sea)food. Come early! In case it's full, there are plenty of other beach restaurants/pubs around. Use Google Maps (you can download the map of this area and use it offline) to get the bus on time. You can take buses heading towards Tripoli from Charles Helou Bus Station or Doura.

A nearer option for swimming if you are staying in Beirut is **Kasliks Military Swimming Pool**. It has both indoor and outdoor pools and you can also swim in the sea. Lockers and showers are available. In the summer it's open all day to the public. You will need your passport to enter, because it's military terrain. The bus from Beirut to Byblos (from Doura) will take you there. Get off at the beginning of Kaslik (on the highway) and walk down to the sea. Ask for the Military Swimming Pool or follow the crowds on warm summer days.

Do not forget to visit the **Phoenician Wall** in the charming city of Batroun. This old civilisation left little traces, but here you will see a big part the protection wall (against the sea) they build. You will find this wall easily if you go to the centre of Batroun and follow the signs or ask anyone. See the photo of the Phoenician Wall on page 84

Tripoli (Trablous)

The second biggest city in Lebanon is, in almost every way, the opposite of Beirut. While the capital is cosmopolitan, has a thriving nightlife and is very mixed in terms of religion, Trablous is a conservative, traditional, Arabic city. The 'Havana of the Middle East' would be an appropriate name, because the many damaged and poorly-maintained buildings do not get in the way of the city's beauty.

The majority of the population is Sunni Muslim, but there are also Alawi Muslims (a branch of Shia Islam) and a small Christian community, in this city that is only 85 kilometres from Beirut.

The Medieval **souq** is a must-see: a remarkable maze of traditional shops under arches that are hundreds of years old. Visit **Charkass Soap Factory**, at Khan el Masriyin (upper floor), where the only remaining soap-maker artisan, Mr. Charkass, still produces soaps in the traditional way. If you look carefully upstairs where the shop is, you can see that Lebanese Jews used to live here. A Star of David is carved into the wooden pillar.

I implore you to pay a visit to the **Great Mosque (Jami al-Kabir)**, built by the Mamaluks on the foundations of a Christian cathedral. Pay special attention to the porch, a superb piece of art. Close to the souq, but uphill, you will find the **Citadel of Raymond the Saint-Gilles** (a crusader castle). It's small, but definitely worth the climb, if only for the view!

Trablous is famous for its sweets. **Abdul Rahman Hallab & Sons** (since 1881), the most renowned baklava makers, originate here. Their beautiful restaurant in Riad el-Sohl street really deserves a visit. And if that's not enough, you will find street vendors, usually older men, selling their delicious homemade sweets on almost every street corner in the heart of the city.

You won't find alcoholic drinks in the Sunni parts of Trablous. In the port city of **al-Mina**, next to Tripoli, you will find some bars and cafés that serve alcoholic beverages. Al-Mina has a diverse population: Sunni Muslims (the majority), Greek-orthodox and, to a lesser extent, Maronite Christians live here among other smaller denominations. The beautiful Greek-Orthodox **Mar Gerges Church** is not always open, but friendly people will help you to get the key. At Christmastime, the decorations surrounding the churches contribute to the special feel of the area. Do not miss out on a pleasant stroll on the Corniche (beach boulevard).

It is easy to get to Trablous from Beirut if you catch a **bus from Doura** (2000 LL, one way). There is also another option: the more luxurious and faster **Connexion bus** from Charles Helou Station (5000 LL, but it runs less frequently). From the central Abdel Hamid Karim Square (with the name of Allah written in big letters in the middle), you will find buses back to Beirut. There is transportation available all night, but from the evening onwards it is limited to minivans only. From the centre of Trablous you can take a taxi or *service* to al-Mina. It is cheap and fast (10 minutes without traffic).

Kadisha Valley

This fabulous place is known as the 'holy valley', a place where Christian Maronites used to hide during Arab invasions in the 7th century AD. You will find many monasteries, caves and beautiful villages here. It is worth mentioning that the first printing press in the Middle East was at Saint Antony in Kadisha Valley. It is located in a monastery in the Valley of the Saints. According to historians, a movable type of printing press was imported from England to the Saint Antonius Monastery in 1585. The first publication was the book of 'Mazameer' dated 1610, which now resides in the University of the Holy Ghost in Kaslik.

Near the village of **Bsharri** lies the famous **Cedar Reserve**, where gigantic cedar trees, that several thousand years old, still stand. Lebanon used to be full of cedar trees, but the wood has been popular since Pharaoic times for ship-building. In Bsharri you can visit the **Gibran Museum**, which honours Lebanon's most famous writer (see chapter VI).

Baalbek

The most stunning **Roman temple complex** you might ever come across is in Baalbek. Naturally, it's on the UNESCO list of protected world heritage. The temple of **Bacchus** is almost intact and bigger than any of its kind in Rome. From the **Jupiter Temple** one row of pillars has survived the many earthquakes this area suffered. Around the two main temples there is an old Roman complex. You can easily imagine how it used to look in its prime. The modern adjacent museum tells the story of Heliopolis (Greek for 'City of the sun'). Please don't forget that you can actually access the Bacchus temple! There are steps down from the main temple complex leading to this giant Roman place of worship. Opening hours: 8:00 to 18:00.

The **Shrine of Sayeeda Khawla** (Hussein's daughter) is one of the most holy places for Shia Muslims, who make the pilgrimage to this place from all over the world. You will find the shrine in the vast, glistening Sayeeda Khawla mosque on the main road next to the car park of the temple complex. It's a palace lined with mirrored tiles, beautiful in its own way. In the middle you will find the shrine. People in this mosque are extremely friendly and happy to explain its importance to visitors. There are separate entrances for men and women and before entering the complex your bag will be checked for security reasons. Please note that entering with shorts is no problem for men, but women should be veiled and have their arms and legs covered.

Along the main road from the exit of the temple complex to the shrine of Hussein's daughter, you will pass the famous **Palmyra Hotel** on your left, where legends like Charles de Gaulle have slept. Nothing has changed in this early 20th century style hotel since it was built. A man who has worked there for the last 40 years is usually present to give a small tour. Do not forget to tip him afterwards (the tours are his livelihood).

In the summer, Baalbek hosts the famous **Baalbeck International Music Festival,** where some of the world's most famous artists have performed against the backdrop of the ancient ruins.

Typical food from this area is the **Safeha** (meat on pastry fresh from the oven) that can be found in small local bakeries.

Baalbek is a **Hezbollah**-dominated city. The population is predominantly Shia but there is also a small Christian minority in the city. Once you enter Baalbek from Beirut you will see many yellow (Hezbollah) flags and portraits of Hassan Nasrallah, the party leader. White minibuses on the Hazmieh highway leaving the capital usually go to Baalbek. If you want a taxi or *service* to bring you to the Hazmieh highway, ask the driver for for al-Sayeed. This is where most people hop on and off the buses. Though cheap (5000 LL, a bit more than 3 USD), some bus drivers drive perilously on the road to Baalbek. I have personally felt quite unsafe in these buses at times. Another, better option is to arrange for a taxi for one day: the price will range from 150 to 200 USD. It usually takes an hour and a half to get to Baalbek from Beirut.

Mleeta Touristic Landmark / 'Hezbollah Museum'

This extraordinary museum lies on top of the mountain, a half hour drive from Sidon. Mleeta means 'where the earth meets the sky', which is a fitting name. The museum embodies Hezbollah's 'victory over Israel', which, according to the movement, started on this mountain.

Known as the 'Hezbollah Museum', Mleeta Tourist Landmark offers you the narrative of the fight against Israel from the perspective of the Shia movement. The southern neighbour invaded Lebanon in 1982 (and even occupied Beirut), but gradually withdrew, under pressure from groups like Hezbollah. In 2000, the last of the Israeli soldiers left Lebanese soil. The two countries have an ongoing dispute about the Shebaa farms. According to Lebanon, these are still under illegal Israeli occupation, while the latter says they are part of the Golan Heights.

Going to Mleeta is an adventure in itself and the well-built and maintained museum is worth the visit. The leader of Hezbollah himself, Hassan Nasrallah, will speak to you through a short film.

You will be shown the places where heavy fighting took place, where mujahedeen hid in a tunnel and, of course, 'the Abyss' in which tanks, military cars and weapons that have been seized from Israeli soldiers are displayed.

The people working in the museum are welcoming and helpful. Whether or not Mleeta Tourist Landmark is propaganda is up to you! The museum is open during the day, until sunset.

From Beirut you can reach Mleeta by **private taxi** (around 75 USD, round trip) **or take a bus** from Cola to Sidon and then a taxi from there (around 40 USD, round trip). In the Shia villages you will see pictures of many martyrs. Be careful when taking pictures and videos, or you might have to spend some time convincing security guards of your good intentions. See also chapter IX in this book.

Sidon (Saida)

The beautiful old souq of Sidon (Saida in Arabic) is very well preserved. You will feel thrown back in time! It's not a place to spend more than a couple of hours though. Personally I love the old chapel where the apostles Peter and Paul met. You can ask for it (Boutros and Bolu are their Arabic names), but you will see signs leading to this medieval chapel while walking around. Ring the bell and somebody will come to open the door. If you are interested in soap: the soap museum in the souq – hard to miss – might attract you. For me, it did not really do the trick.

Sidon, a mainly Sunni city, used to have the biggest Jewish population of the country: 3500 people according to the 1932 census. The old synagogue is still present. According to news reports, a Palestinian family now lives in this rundown building. In 2012 two orthodox rabbis visited the place and prayed inside. You will find the synagogue in the old Jewish quarter Harat al-Yahud, next to the souq.

Apart from the old sea castle, Sidon does not have much to offer tourists.

Minibuses to Saida leave from Cola Bus Station, but might take the old coastal road. The coaches of the Lebanese Bus Company take the highway, and are much faster.

Tyre (Sour)

Better known as Sour in Lebanon, this southern city is famous for its beaches and archaeological sites. Why not combine the two on a day trip? Start at the port in the small, old, Christian town. You will recognise it from the coloured houses. At the port you will find excellent fish restaurants. Keep following the coastline, turn left, leaving al-Mina and head inland: you will encounter the first Roman columns and graves. However, the best is still to come. Take a taxi or *service* to the famous Hippodrome and beautiful Roman arch, which are located on the other side of the city. This is the highlight of the tour. After this, you can have a swim at the excellent beaches of Sour.

Take a direct bus to Tyre from the Kuwait Embassy (close to Cola Bus Station).

LGBTQI-travellers

The good news first: Beirut has a lot to offer LGBTQI travellers. There are plenty of gay-friendly bars, clubs and restaurants. And for the more adventurous among you, there are saunas, cinemas and cruising areas (all for men only). However, although they are known to be frequented mainly by a LGBTQI crowd, none of the places is officially a gay venue. You will not see rainbow flags, bear symbols etc. in Beirut. Discreet behaviour is expected in these places, however this is not always respected.

All 'gay-friendly places' are just ordinary bars, clubs etc. that just happen to attract a quite specific crowd. Anything more than dancing close together is not allowed in the two big clubs, Posh and Projekt. Special guards on the dance floor (usually brawny guys wearing a black T-shirt) intervene if people do not behave 'decently'. You will feel safe actually and it's good to know that the police have never raided bars, clubs or restaurants that are friendly to gay people.

The most popular bar is **Bardo,** a friendly and classy bar where people dance late at night. It's next to Haigazian University on Mexico Street. Bardo also offers good food. **Dark Box** (Monot Street, turn left halfway up, if you are coming from Gouraud) is for transvestites and their lovers, **Kahwet al-Franj,** friendly café and restaurant for bears (at the border of Mar Mikhael. Take Armenia Street and turn right before the bridge over the river. You will see it after one minute on your right).

In **Em Nazih** you will find mostly straight people, but in an interesting mix which includes foreigners and queer people. Drinks are cheap, the food is good and affordable and the staff is friendly. Em Nazih can be found in Gemmayze (Rue Pasteur, walk down the steps next to Lodge) and in Hamra. **T-Marboota** in Hamra has a great outside terrace, excellent food and also attracts a mixed crowd. See above (bars and restaurants) for directions.

Lesbians might prefer to go to **Madame Om,** which is next to Em Nazih. A beautiful old-style Beirut residence houses this pub, which also attracts a male crowd. You can find this bar easily if you take the steps up from the rear terrace of Em Nazih. Madame Om is in the old building on the second floor. You can also get there from Rue Pasteur: walk in the direction of downtown and turn right after the petrol station. The building will be in front of you.

For **hammams** (saunas), old, rundown cinemas and outdoor cruising, it's a different story, though the times the police have raided these places are rare and the reasons are diverse. Outdoor cruising, needless to say, is dangerous. If you want to be on the safe side (and you do) you can go to the **marina of Dbaye**. At the very beginning there are mostly men cruising around. Here people exchange phone numbers for later contact – all discreetly of course. Never try anything out in the open (not even a kiss), because there are many (sometimes undercover) police controls.

There are **no gay hammams** in Lebanon, but some of them attract a LGBTQI crowd. Massages are also offered. **Sherazade**, close to the football stadium in **Bourj Hammoud**, is a place where you can enjoy the steam room, dry sauna and hot tub. It's the most frequented hammam and can get quite packed, especially at weekends. Sherazade is open from 15:00 until after midnight. As in all other saunas it offers body massage (be sure you know the price prior to your massage). Directions: walk from Snack Garo on Masaken passed the stadium, at the second street to the left you will find the hammam.

The other Beirut hammam, **al-Bakawat (formerly al-Agha)**, in Verdun, next to the Bristol Hotel, you enter via an underground entrance. It's more frequented during the day, but not usually busy. Good for relaxing.

In **Tripoli** you will find **al-Abed**, Lebanon's oldest hammam that is still in use. It was built in 1700 and has retained many of its original features. This hammam still offers 'ritual' cleaning before marriage. You will be amazed by the classical entrance. Even if you do not want to take a bath you can have a quick look inside. The entrance is from the souq, close to the famous soap factory, Khan al-Saboun. The Tripoli souq is like a maze, so you might need to ask for directions.

And now for the bad news: 'unnatural sexual behaviour' is punishable by law in Lebanon and people have been prosecuted based on this law. However, there is jurisprudence that stipulates that this law doesn't apply to sex between people of the same sex. Still, as long as the law is not withdrawn, LGBTQI people are not protected by the State. It's unlikely the situation will change in the near future, because equal rights for LGBTQI people are not on the political agenda. Moreover, leaders of the religious communities oppose such a thing.

Seeing what Beirut already has to offer to LGBTQI travellers, Lebanon misses great opportunities. If gay people had equal rights, many more tourists would come to Lebanon. It could become the 'Berlin of the Middle East', bringing in money and employment and most of all, happiness for all the people who are still in the closet in Lebanon.

Useful information

- For **women travelling alone** Lebanon is known to be a safe country. Be extra vigilant at night or when taking taxis from the street. Harassment of women on the street is extremely rare. In conservative areas it's wise, mainly out of respect, to dress more conservatively (avoid short skirts and low-cut tops for example). Except for entering mosques, women are never required to cover their heads.
- The **Lebanese Pound** (LBP, also known as Lebanese Lira) is the official currency of Lebanon, but **US dollars** are accepted everywhere, even in the smallest shops and villages. The rate is fixed at 1500 LBP to 1 USD. It's easy to convert from dollars to lira: you take half the number dollars and add them to the original number. Then multiply by 1000. Thus 20 USD: 10 +20= 30, so 30.000 LBP. If you pay by credit card in restaurants or shops you will be asked in which currency you would like to pay. If you have a USD account, you should always pay in this currency. In recent years, Europeans with a EUR account have gained slightly by paying in USD.
- **Hospitals** and **doctors** are very good in Lebanon. Patients from all over the Middle East go to Lebanon for special treatments. In

Beirut you will find many hospitals. The private hospital **Saint George** (or Roum) has an excellent reputation. However, there are many good options. Just make sure you are insured when you travel. If it is not an emergency, private hospitals will not help you unless you are insured or pay beforehand.

- **Taking shared taxis** is not always easy for foreigners. Once the *service* drivers (pronounced: ser-vees) sense you are unfamiliar with the system they will tell you that you are in a private taxi, which has much higher rates. Sometimes they will only announce this once you have arrived at your destination! So check from the start of the ride if you are entering a *service* and just pay the fixed rate (see above under 'Transportation' for the rates). If the driver becomes angry, do not be intimidated. I have sometimes just gently left the car, leaving the money behind, while the driver was cursing at me. Or, if it was late at night, I have given a bit extra, just to calm him down.

Warnings

- The security situation in Lebanon can change quickly. **Check the local news before you travel.** Naharnet.com is an English-language news website on Lebanon that highlights the most important developments. Also the search engine in Twitter (for example #Tripoli #Baalbek or spelled as Baalback etc.) can be useful.
- You will not be allowed to enter Lebanon if your passport contains **Israeli stamps**. And even though Israel is known to not stamp passports any more, be aware that baggage tags (for example of an El Al flight to Tel Aviv) can be used as a reason to deny you entry into Lebanon. If your passport shows that you were born in Israel you might not get in to Lebanon. Being Jewish or having a Jewish name is (in general) not a problem, though it might raise questions at the border. Remember, Judaism is one of the 18 official 'sects' (religions) of Lebanon.

- **Checkpoints** are everywhere in Lebanon: take your passport with you if you travel outside Beirut and when inside Beirut, store a picture of your passport in your phone.
- **Traffic can be very dangerous**, especially in Beirut. Do not assume cars will stop when you cross the street, not even when the light is green for pedestrians. Be extremely careful.
- **Homosexuality** is not accepted in Lebanese society and 'unnatural sex' is punishable by law. If you are gay (and are travelling with your partner), you should keep this in mind when you are in public areas.
- In some sensitive areas (such as Hezbollah-controlled Shiite neighbourhoods), **taking pictures** can arouse suspicion, even if it is a picture of a tree or a stray cat. You might be asked to delete pictures. Never take photos of the Lebanese army or their buildings. In places where LGBTQI people gather you are sometimes not allowed to film or take photos (for example in club Posh). Be careful anyway when taking pictures in these kinds of places, because it can be very dangerous for LGBTQI people if other people later see them on social media in a 'gay' setting.
- **Remove sensitive information from your phone or laptop.** And remember: what might seem innocent in the US, Australia or Europe can be seen as provocation in Lebanon. If you have called people in Israel from your home country and their number appears in your contacts list, this might raise suspicion and can bring trouble ('Are you a spy'?). The Lebanese police do not have the right to look into your phone unless they have a reason to suspect you, but Hezbollah will – if they think it's necessary for local security – ask you to open your phone for them. You cannot blame them. Their community has been hit many times by car bombs and air raids.

Chef Michel Yammine

'Lebanese food is a celebration of life'

What are the secrets of Lebanese cuisine? And is it true that the best food in the Middle East comes from Lebanon? All these questions (and many more) I put to top Lebanese chef, Michel Yammine, who is an ambassador of his country's food in the Netherlands.

For the people who do not know you: please introduce yourself. Who are you?
My name is Michel, and Lebanese food is my passion. I am the owner and founder of 'Food by Michel'. After working for a long time for top Lebanese restaurants, I decided to start my own catering company. One of my goals was to put Lebanese food in the spotlight in the Netherlands. That's why I attend many open air markets, like the Zeeburg market in Amsterdam.'

There are not many Lebanese people in the Netherlands. Is this an advantage for you as a chef?
Lebanese food is becoming more and more well-known. Recently quite a few Lebanese restaurants have opened in Holland. In fact it's an advantage for me, because people will look out more for catering and Lebanese cooking workshops.

For those unfamiliar with Lebanese food: what is typically Lebanese? And how is it different from the cuisine of other countries in the Middle East?
Lebanese food belongs to the Mediterranean kitchen. There are lots of similarities among these kitchens, but also differences. Sometimes unbelievable: with the same ingredients you can create different foods sometimes. Compare Italian pasta, Lebanese *armachta* and Greek *pastisio* for example.

A unique cultural history has helped to make Lebanese food the most popular of all Middle Eastern cuisines. The similarities among them cannot be denied, but Lebanese food remains special and distinguished. Our dishes are often prepared and seasoned differently.

Lebanese cuisine is unique because it combines the sophistication of European cuisines with the exotic ingredients of the Orient. It includes copious amounts of garlic and olive oil seasoned with lemon juice. We rarely use butter or cream in our savoury dishes. Lebanese cuisine focuses on herbs, spices, and fresh ingredients.

A meal usually starts with *mezzes*, a wide selection of hot and cold appetisers. For example, there are salads such as the world-famous tabouleh, fattoush and raheb salad. Famous *mezzes* also include: hummus, baba ghannouj, moutabbal, labneh with garlic and olive oil, deep-fried patties or falafel, mujaddara (made of lentils), sambousek or fatayer, small pies filled with cheese, spinach or meat, stuffed vine leaves, shanklish, white cheeses, sausages, and kibbeh (lamb meat with bulgur wheat).

There are as many as forty *mezze* dishes that can be served at the same time, which makes it a unique culinary experience. Sometimes these *mezze* dishes constitute the whole meal.

The main course usually consists of grilled red meat, chicken or fish served with cooked rice and bread, a staple food in Lebanon. Flat bread or pitta is served with almost every meal. Literally not a meal in Lebanon is eaten without bread.

Desserts include a wide variety of sweets such as baklava, often containing pistachio nuts and drizzled with rose-water syrup (whereas Greek baklava contains walnuts and is drizzled with honey), knefeh, katayef, maamoul, karabige, as well as fresh fruits, dried fruits, and nuts.

At the end of a typical meal, black coffee (Turkish style) is generally served. Coffee is a big deal in Lebanon; it is actually served throughout the day. Lebanese coffee is strong, thick, and often flavoured with cardamom.

Mediterranean countries are famous for their aniseed-flavoured drinks. In the south of France, they drink Pastis. In Italy, it's Sambuca and in Greece, they drink Ouzo. Arak, our anise-flavoured liqueur, is the national Lebanese drink and is usually served with a traditional convivial meal.

Another ancient and traditional drink in Lebanon is wine. Lebanese wines (Ksara, Kefraya, Massaya, Château Musar, Ixsir, Marsyas) are famous around the world. In addition to its many renowned wineries, Lebanon also boasts a number of breweries, and local beers are very popular.

The Lebanese food is a celebration of life; it is fresh, flavourful, diverse, invigorating, and in a class of its own. The genius of it lies in its simplicity, and the food is a product of the Earth and the sea – the Mediterranean Sea.

Where do you think people should definitely go to experience the real Lebanese taste in Lebanon?
There are the usual landmark restaurants such as Bourj El Hamam or Restaurant Fakhredine in Broummana. There are also Lebanese restaurants with a modern twist such as Liza or Babel in Beirut. Alternatively for an authentic Lebanese experience, a village restaurant on a hill is perfect; Tawlet in Beiteddine and Gemmeyze are fine examples of such an experience. And let me not forget restaurant Yammine, owned by my family, in Nabee al-Safa. It's a traditional restaurant in the Lebanese mountains. A truly great experience.

www.foodbymichel.com

Biography
Born: 4 August 1974 in Lebanon
Lives in: Amsterdam
Profession: Lebanese Chef
Contact: Foodbymichel@yahoo.com
(003161445943)
www.foodbymichel.com

Disclaimer:

The individuals mentioned in this book are real people. However, the names of Tofik, Samir and André have been changed in order to protect their identity. In addition, I have chosen to omit the exact location of the 'hidden synagogue'.

Acknowledgments

Many thanks to:

- Diederik Rodenburg for his tremendous effort in translating the original Dutch version of this book into English. Ayesha de Sousa did the final editing, for which I am very grateful.

- Elie and Tofik for their wonderful hospitality. Your house feels like home to me. I have written so many stories from the balcony of your beautiful apartment. *Merci ktir!* (many thanks)

- Linda van Tilburg for her editing of the original Dutch book and her continuous support of my work.

- My dear friend Abed who showed me so many (secret) places in Lebanon.

- Wassim Beaineh and Camille Karout for their critical look at my work.

- Thank you, Lebanon, for hosting me time and time again!

Made in the USA
Middletown, DE
17 April 2019